On Earth as it is In Heaven

Priscilla

Be Blessed = Supremely
Happy so as to be
envied By others As
They see your lif joy,
satisfaction, salvation
Regardless of your
circumstances!

Rodney

Published by WordCrafts Press
Cody, Wyoming 82414
www.wordcrafts.net

On Earth
as it is
In Heaven

RODNEY BOYD

WordCrafts

CONTENTS

DEDICATION

As always, this book is dedicated to my lovely wife Brenda who has traveled with me on this road for 45+ years. From the moment when you stepped into that garage where the band that I was playing with was rehearsing, I knew that you were the one. Thank God that you eventually knew it also.

To Phillip Boyd (my son) and Jamie (his wife) who bless me beyond comprehension. A man cannot ask for more than these two.

This book is also dedicated to those who are sick and tired of being sick and tired and who have been convinced that it is the will of God for them to be sick and tired.

I also want to give a shout out to all of those who have attended the Ruminator Sunday School Class where I taught for 27 years in some form or fashion the principles found in this book.

I want to also dedicate this book on healing to a strong woman of faith, a teacher of the Word of God, a mentor to many, and a lady who encouraged me to continue in the Word of God concerning healing—Susan Cleveland. This dear lady has been healed by God many times of life threatening dis-eases but this time she stepped into the presence of the Healer for ultimate healing. It was a win/win situation for her. Bless her family including her husband Rick Cleveland. In the '70s I had the honor of being in their wedding.

Last but not least I want to dedicate this book to Emerson Grace Boyd. At the time of this writing, it has been almost a year (June 15th 2017) since I had a stroke (not mine, I don't claim it) with a prognosis of death (if the swelling of the brain did not go down). Death was imminent, but the Lord intervened, and on May 21st 2018, Monday night at 8:40 (give or take a few minutes) Emerson Grace was born, and I was able to hold our first granddaughter in my arms. Thank God for healing on earth as it is in heaven.

INTRODUCTION

This book, as with my other books, has been years in the making. It flows out of teachings presented in the Ruminator Sunday School Class that I taught for 27 years, my work experiences of 30+ years in the medical field as a Speech-Language Pathologist, and multiple practical applications of praying for the sick and dying in multiple settings.

While we focus on healing in this book, the principles that I outline apply to anything involved in our lives here on earth as we seek how it is in heaven. It can be healing physically, or provision financially, or emotional stability, or any area where we regulate ourselves and conduct ourselves by faith and not by sight or things revealed to the senses (II Corinthians 5:7). Anything that involves our spirits, our souls, and our bodies can be applied (I Thessalonians 5:23).

There are two key verses for the foundation of this book.

"Thy kingdom come, Thy will be done on earth as it is in heaven."

Matthew 6:10

"How God anointed and consecrated Jesus of Nazareth

with the [Holy] Spirit and with strength and ability and power; how He went about doing good and, in particular, curing all who were harassed and oppressed by [the power of] the d-evil, for God was with Him."

Acts 10:38, AMP
with emphasis mine

There is a verse found in Acts 20:27 where Paul speaks of a thing called "the full/whole counsel/purpose of God."

"For I never shrank or kept back or fell short from declaring to you the whole purpose and plan and counsel of God."

Acts 20:27, AMP

As we look for the "will of God on earth as it is in heaven," realize that *no one can know every intent and purpose of God* for our lives, but we will be looking at *what is revealed to us and walk in the revealed.*

"The secret things belong to the Lord our God, but the things revealed belong to us and to our sons forever, that we may observe all the words of this law."

Deuteronomy 29:29

I wrote this book because I am sick and tired of being sick and tired, and I am sick and tired of seeing so many people who are sick and tired of being sick and tired and have been duped into believing that it is God's will being done on earth by them being sick and tired and overwhelmed by the d-evil. Over the ages there have been many books written, many sermons preached, and many teachings about healings, and well, *this certainly is another one.*

There is no denying that sickness, disease, afflictions, and addictions are real. There is no denying that strong men and women of the faith—true believers—get sick, die in their sickness, become addicted and possessed by the things of the flesh. This book is not designed to debate whether or not *it is God's will to heal or if He still heals or even it God is concerned about the affairs of mankind and intervenes on our behalf by the breath of our prayers.* We engage God in our lives by *faith.* Faith does not come by your experience, your religious heritage, your traditions, your goodness, your merit, who you know, what you know, or what you have done, but *faith comes by hearing and hearing by the Word of God* or words concerning Christ (Romans 10:17).

This book is not based on your *what ifs,* or your *buts,* or you praying for someone and they died, or horror stories of someone standing in faith and not taking their medicine, or worse some adult refusing to give their child medicine and the child died. This book is not based on dispensations of healing starting and stopping, or if the last apostle died, or if the church was established and now there is no need for these things, or if the final version of the Bible was canonized (authorized when books collected) and we need no more revelation. It is not based on *the cessation of God in our lives.*

All of your questions about healing will *not be answered* by me in this book. Why? Because I don't know all the answers. I lean heavily on Deuteronomy 29:29:

"The secret things belong to the Lord our God, but those

things which are revealed belong to us and to our children forever; that we may do all the words of this law."

I am not approaching this book from a *non-biased perspective.* I am approaching it from a *very biased perspective.* It is designed for those *who have given up hope,* for those *who have received bad reports from their physicians, those who wished that healing was true but know it's not* because they prayed and they are still sick. This book is for those who may be strong in their faith about their salvation but are weak in their faith about healing. It is for those who believe they deserve to be sick and believe that God is teaching them a lesson by causing cancer, diabetes, or any other sickness and disease to come upon them. This book is designed to help you to restrain and retrain your thoughts, words, and actions as you are faced with the impossibilities of life.

"Unrestrained thoughts (what you think) produces unrestrained words (what you say) resulting in unrestrained actions (what you do)." (Kenneth Copeland—How to Discipline Your Flesh)

I hope this book will help us *restrain our thoughts* concerning sickness, disease, finances, world events, inter-personal relationships, and we will begin to *speak and do* the Word of God concerning everything in our lives. In a world filled with sickness, disease, pain, hurting, poverty, distress, fear, anxiety, death, and dying we point out that Jesus is the same (1) yesterday (2) today (3) and yes, forever as He went about and still goes about (through His people) (a) doing good (b) healing all who were and still are oppressed by the d-evil (little d...he does not deserve a capital letter) for God was with Him (and us) *by the anointing* (the yoke destroying, burden lifting, oppression removing, healing power of the Holy Spirit) (Hebrews 13:8; Acts 10:38 with emphasis mine). When you read the Gospels (The Good News According to Matthew, Mark, Luke, and John you will see 40 incidents of Jesus doing the will of the Father on earth as it was in heaven using 10 different methods of delivery. Every time you see Jesus healing or delivering he was *destroying the works of the d-evil* (I John 3:8) and removing *oppression of the d-evil* (Acts 10:38). And that was just what was written in the record (aka the Bible) not including what was not written (John 21:25).

In a world with 100,000 diseases, filled with the latest medical equipment, the most educated physicians in the world, the most current medicinal breakthroughs, holistic healing, and the highest level of intellectual pursuits we are still a *world-wide sick society*. In this book *I don't deny the validity of* physicians, medicine, diet, holistic medicines, herbs, education, etc. but that is *not the focus of this book*. You are holding in your hands a book designed to take a look at not only *healing* but anything involved with what God has for us. My hope is that as you read through this book, as you look up the Scriptures, as you ruminate and meditate on God's thoughts about healing, that faith will come, that hope will rise up, that you will leave the comfort of the pews of traditions, go out and as the body of Christ begin to be an extension of this *Jesus who has not changed*, who is *the same, yesterday, today and yes, forever* (Hebrews 13:8).

When Jesus was here on planet earth for 33 years, three of those years were ministering to the needs of the people. When He was crucified, died, buried, rose from the dead, and went back to the Father, the mission of bringing the will of the Father on earth as it is in heaven did not stop. Jesus sent the Holy Spirit who was *another* (*allos*—Greek word for another) Comforter, one of the same kind (allos) to give us the commission and power to carry on the mission. Jesus left planet earth and sent back One of the same kind. I hope this book will bless and encourage you and that faith will come for you so you can pass it on.

As I am writing this book, I am a year and a half on the other side of having a stroke. During that time I was in the intensive care unit for nine days of which I do not remember anything. I was surrounded constantly by Brenda who prayed for me and by many friends who came to the hospital to support Brenda and lift me up. For years I have taught in Sunday school, in the Ruminator Sunday School Class, that if I am ever in the hospital, do not come see me with doubt or negative unbelief, but come full of faith and speaking and praying healing for me. I am proud, in a humble way, to say this is what happened. At one point the doctors called in my family to make end of life decisions and prepare them for the worse. They were told that if the swelling in my brain did not reduce, then I would die.

The two most faith-filled words are, *"But God."* I was on the brink of death, *"But God"* intervened. I continue to improve and my thoughts about God and His supernatural healing have *not diminished* but have strengthened. Since I began conceiving and writing this book on healing I have experienced a stroke, was in the intensive care unit for nine days and in a regular room for three days, dealt with being physically weak, emotionally despondent, not motivated, had reduced creativity, and overall was in a funk. Thanks to the *prayers of the saints* and the *diligence of the physicians*, I have been declared a miracle. When your physician in the hospital states that you are a miracle, then they are in agreement with me—*I am a miracle*.

Needless to say, I am now a chapter in this book entitled, *What Do You Do When You Believe and Teach Healing and Then You Get Sick?*

I posted on Facebook (while I was in ICU) on my author page once I was able—"You know that you are an author, when you have a stroke and go to the hospital and consider you're hospitalization as research for your book on healing."

As you read this book, my prayer is that as you face *anything in your life*, that your faith will be built up and you will be able to come through it healed, delivered, set free, prosperous, and living the abundant life.

After each chapter there is a homework section. The last chapter is a workbook with 42 incidences of Jesus healing in the Gospels. This book should be read with a Bible, pen, and notebook to record your personal thoughts and revelations.

Rodney Lewis Boyd, 2017

FOREWORD

The genesis of this book is the Kingdom of God and how everything in our lives as believers in the death, burial, and resurrection of Jesus the Christ, emanates from the Kingdom. Christ Jesus does not revolve around us or our thrones (the rightful place of a king), but everything in our lives revolves around the King of the Kingdom. A Kingdom is defined in the Greek Language as:

KINGDOM: basileia (*bas-il-i'-ah*)=From G935; properly *royalty*, that is, (abstractly) *rule*, or (concretely) a *realm* (literally or figuratively): - kingdom, + reign. G935: basileus bas-il-yooce'=Probably from G939 (through the notion of a *foundation* of power); a *sovereign* (abstractly, relatively or figuratively G939: basis (bas'-ece)=From bainō (to walk); a pace ("base"), that is, (by implication) the foot: - foot.
1. Royalty
2. A realm
3. A reign
4. A foundation of power
5. A sovereign
6. A pace (base)
7. Foot

A Kingdom is defined in the Hebrew Language as:

KINGDOM: malkûth malkûth malkûyâh (mal-kooth', mal-kooth', mal-koo-yaw')=From H4427; a rule; concretely a dominion: - empire, kingdom, realm, reign, royal. H4427: mâlak maw-lak'= A primitive root; to reign; inceptively to ascend the throne; causatively to induct into royalty; hence (by implication) to take counsel: - consult, X indeed, be (make, set a, set up) king, be (make) queen, (begin to, make to) reign (-ing), rule, X surely.

In the Old Testament a kingdom is
1. A rule
2. Concretely a dominion
3. Empire
4. To reign
5. To ascend the throne
6. To induct into royalty
7. To take counsel

Where there is a Kingdom, there is a king, and where there is a king there are subjects who have subjected their will to the King's will. Earthly kingdoms are usually established by overthrow, but the Kingdom of God is where willing subjects yield their will to the King's will. For further study on the concept of the Kingdom of God I would recommend:

Pondering (s) TOO by Wayne Berry
WordCrafts Press 2019
The King and You by Bob Mumford
Fleming H. Revell Company 1974
The Secret Kingdom by Pat Robertson
Word Publishing 1992

The Unshakeable Kingdom and The Unchanging Person by
E. Stanley Jones
  Abigdon Press 1972
  Cosmic Initiative by Jack Taylor
  Whitaker House 2017
  Understanding the Kingdom (Preparing for Kingdom Experience and Expansion by Myles Munroe
  Destiny Image 2006

KINGDOM PRINCIPLES

While this book deals primarily with healing, the principles involved can be applied to anything in our lives concerning Kingdom living. Every area of our lives including, physical, mental, emotional, and spiritual healing, finances, relationships with others including family members, politics, (fill in the blank of anything in your life that concerns you.)

As I view the Kingdom, I see two aspects:

1. The Kingdom of Heaven
2. The Kingdom of God

Both Kingdoms are of God, but I view of Heaven as the headquarters of the Kingdom and of God as the outpost here on earth.

> *"Thy kingdom (rule, reign, foundation of power) come, Thy will (wish, desire) be done on earth (the outposts of heaven) as it is in heaven (headquarters)."*

> Matthew 6:10
> with emphasis and additions mine

The purpose of Kingdom living on planet earth is to

introduce and enforce the principle of the headquarters.

Notice the interlinking aspect of the Kingdom and the King's will being manifested on the outpost. When I check in with headquarters via prayer and the code book (the Bible) I do not find cancer, diabetes, strokes, arthritis, migraine headaches (fill in the blank of any sickness, dis-ease, dis-comfort, dys-function) in heaven, so I begin to speak/pray/confess/declare the Kingdom will be here on earth.

Romans 14:17 defines what the Kingdom of God is and what it is not.

> *"[After all] the kingdom of God is not a matter of [getting the] food and drink [one likes], but instead it is righteousness (that state which makes a person acceptable to God) and [heart], peace and joy in the Holy Spirit."*
>
> Romans 14:17, AMP

When you put together the definition of the kingdom in the Greek language and Romans 14:17 you get:

> *"Thy rule, reign, foundation of power of righteousness, peace and joy in the Holy Ghost, come and Thy wish and desire be done (accomplished and manifested) on earth as it is in heaven."*
>
> Matthew 6:10, Romans 14:17
> with emphasis and addition mine

One last thing. What is this thing called "the will of God," or more importantly, what is this thing called "the Kingdom will of God?" I am of the opinion that you cannot separate the Kingdom from the King's will (wish/desire). Bob Mumford in his book The King and You clarifies the word, *will*:

"We need to understand that there are two different words used in the Greek for our English word, *will*, as it is used throughout Scripture. One is boulema, the other is thelema. Boulema means the eternal counsels of God which are unfolding through the ages, His purpose, His determination (His will). It (His will) is going to be done whether you and I like it or not. God's intention will come to pass. However, thelema which means God's wish or desire, most often depends upon the response of each individual for fulfillment." (Bob Mumford, *The King and You*)

For me this clears up the misconception of what appears to be conflicting wills. At times it looks as if God is schizophrenic, or a God on the level of Greek or Roman gods, toying with people on planet earth. Mumford continues:

"Referring again to Jesus' words in Matthew 6:10, "Thy kingdom come, thy will be done in earth as it is in heaven," do you see this prayer brings the wish or desire (thelema) into an earthly setting? Without getting theological or complicated, could you understand when I say God's will (His wish, desire) is not being done on earth as it is in heaven? This has nothing to do with the eternal counsels of the Almight, but rather His intimate intervention in the affairs of our lives. It is not the will (wish, desire) of God that divorce, family problems, poverty, sickness, continue in the world (unchallenged, not resisted). God sent His King, in the power of the Kingdom, to change and adjust the situation to conform to this desire. Examine for a moment the demonized man who could neither see not speak. Surely this is not the wish of our God?! (Bob Mumford, *The King and You*)

So this brings me back to the foundation of power for this book, *On Earth as it is In Heaven*, that the will of God is that "no one perish" or be sick. His will on earth as it is in heaven is freedom from sin and all the entrapments that accompany sin. This is the Kingdom will of God for us. Combine this with Acts 10:38 and we see the will of God from headquarters manifested on the outpost of earth.

> *"You know of Jesus of Nazareth (the Healer) how God anointed Him (for the purpose of destroying the works of the d-evil) with the Holy Spirit (the person) and with power (duNAmis, dynamic ability) and how he (Jesus) went about (for three years demonstrating the will of God) doing good (not bad) and healing (bringing people from the point of sickness to the point of not being sick any longer) all (over 40 incidences in the Gospels of healing) who were harassed and oppressed by the d-evil (not God), for God was with Him (Jesus, Immanuel, God with us)."*
>
> Acts 10:38, AMP
> with emphasis and additions mine

When you put together the definition of the kingdom in the Greek language and Romans 14:17 you get:

> *"Thy rule, reign, foundation of power of righteousness, peace and joy in the Holy Ghost, come and Thy wish and desire be done (accomplished and manifested) on earth as it is in heaven."*
>
> Matthew 6:10, Romans 14:17
> with emphasis and addition mine

Now, get out your Bibles, get a notebook and pen, and be ready to have your faith increased concerning the Kingdom of God and His Kingdom will on earth as it is in heaven.

CHAPTER ONE

THE PROBLEM

"There are approximately *100,000* known diseases worldwide." (World Health Organization) There is an estimated shortage of 4.3 million physicians, nurses, and other health workers worldwide. The WHO produced a list of countries with a "Human Resources for Health crisis." In these countries, there are only 1.13 doctors for every 1,000 people.

"As of August 2018, the total population of the world exceeds 7.63 billion people, and this number is continuing to grow each day." (*World Population Review*)

"The human body is made of 11 important organ systems, including the circulatory, respiratory, digestive, excretory, nervous, and endocrine systems. They also include the immune, integumentary, skeletal, muscle, and reproductive systems. The systems work together to maintain a functioning human body." (*What Are The Organ Systems Of The Human Body?* www.study.com)

Ancient biblical texts lists various curses related to the human body found in Deuteronomy 28:15-61. These various sicknesses and diseases are not considered to be blessings from God but curses as a violation of the Law.

"Now it shall be, if you will diligently obey the Lord your God, being careful to do all His commandments, which I

*command you today, the Lord your God will set you high
above all nations of the earth. All these blessings shall come
upon you and overtake you if you obey the Lord your God."*

Deuteronomy 28:1

*"He sent His Word and healed them, and delivered them
from their destructions."*

Psalm 107:20

*"Surely He has borne our griefs (sicknesses, weaknesses,
and distresses) and carried our sorrows and pains [of pun-
ishment], yet we [ignorantly] considered Him stricken, and
afflicted by God [as if with leprosy], but He was wounded
for our transgressions, He was bruised for our guilt and
iniquities; the chastisement [needful to obtain] peace and
well-being for us was upon Him, and with the stripes [that
wounded] Him we are healed and made whole."*

Isaiah 53:4-5, AMP

*"Bless (affectionately, gratefully praise) the Lord, O my
soul, and forget not [one of] all His benefits—Who forgives
[everyone of] all your iniquities, Who heals [each one of]
all your diseases."*

Psalm 103:2-3, AMP

*"How God anointed and consecrated Jesus of Nazareth
with the [Holy] Spirit and with strength and ability and
power; how He went about doing good and, in particular,
curing all who were harassed and oppressed by [the power
of the d-evil], for God was with Him."*

Acts 10:38, AMP

17

HOMEWORK

1. What are the two keys to overtaking blessings coming? (Deuteronomy 28:1)

a.

b.

2. What is the intensity of obedience required? (Deuteronomy 28:1)

3. Where will you be set up and at what level? (Deuteronomy 28:1)

The promises of blessing are then compared with the curse.

> "But (in contrast to the blessings) it shall come about, if you will not obey the Lord your God, to observe to do all His commandments and His statutes with which I charge you today, that all these curses shall come upon you and overtake you."
>
> Deuteronomy 28:15

4. To what are the promises of blessings contrasted? (Deuteronomy 28:15)

5. What are the two keys to bringing on curses? (Deuteronomy 28:15)

6. Curses will come upon you, but what else will the curses do? (Deuteronomy 28:15)

Everything from *inflammation of the joints* to *plague* to *hemorrhoids (emrods)* is considered to be *a curse and not a blessing.* Wow, inflammation of the hemorrhoids (emrods gives a whole new meaning to "*roid rage.*"

As of 2017 (the time of writing of this book) there were approximately *30,000 known diseases* worldwide and in

Deuteronomy there are but a *few sicknesses listed* as a curse. But God covers anything that is not named with Deuteronomy 28:61.

> *"Also every sickness and every plague, which is not written in the book of this law, the Lord will bring (allow because of disobedience) on you until you are destroyed."*
>
> Deuteronomy 28:61

7. How many of the sicknesses and plagues are covered in the book that are not written? (Deuteronomy 28:16)
8. How long will the sicknesses and plagues be allowed to come on you? (Deuteronomy 28:61)

We will cover the roots of sickness, dis-ease, dis-comfort, dys-function, and death in the chapter entitled: *ON EARTH (PRE-FALL)*. The good news is that Jesus the Christ hung on a tree (aka the cross) in our place so that we could go from being cursed to being blessed. We will look at that more a little later. (Galatians 3:10:14) The bottom line is that with the cross we have a choice like they had pre-cross.

> *"I call heaven and earth to witness against you today, that I have set before you, life and death, the blessing and the curse. So choose life in order that you may live, you and your descendants."*
>
> Deuteronomy 30:18

9. Who has God called as a witness concerning blessings and curses? (Deuteronomy 30:18)
10. What are the four choices that are set before you? (Deuteronomy 30:18)

a.
b.
c.
d.

In our next chapter we will look at the request for God's Kingdom (rule, reign, foundation of power) to come on earth as it is in heaven.

CHAPTER TWO

THY KINGDOM COME

"Thy Kingdom come Thy will be done on earth as it is in heaven."

Matthew 6:10

There are two places where we are introduced to what has come to be known as "The Lord's Prayer." One is found in Matthew 6:8-13 and the other in Luke 11:2-4.

While it is known as the Lord's Prayer, it really was the Lord instructing the disciples on how to pray at their request. The *real* Lord's Prayers are found in various places including:

- Early Morning/Lonely Place   Mark 1:35
- Praise Prayer   Matthew 11:25-26
- Mountain Side Prayer   Matthew 14:23
- All Night Prayer   Luke 6:12
- Prayers For Peter   Luke 22:31-32
- Kneeling Fervent Prayer   Luke 22:39-44
- Forgiving Prayer   Luke 23:34
- Benefit For Others Prayers   John 11:41-42
- Troubled Prayers   John 12:27-28
- Pray For Those Who Believe   John 17:1-26
- Prayers and Supplications   Hebrews 5:7

Jesus was a man of prayer who knew how to connect with His *"Father who art in heaven."* (Matthew 6:9)

In the Gospel of Luke passage (Luke 11:1-4), Jesus was praying in a *certain place,* and when He had finished praying one of His disciples asked Him to teach them to pray. Now, Jesus had just got through praying, and you would think the request would be for *Him to teach them* how to pray like *He prayed.* It was pointed out to me once that those must have been some impressive prayers from John and his disciples to make them (the disciples) want Jesus to teach them to pray *like John's disciples.* Here is the prayer found in Matthew 6:9-13:

> *Our Father who art in heaven*
> *Hallowed be Thy name*
> *Thy kingdom come*
> *Thy will be done*
> *On earth as it is in heaven*
> *Give us this day our daily bread*
> *And forgive us our debts, as we also have forgiven our debtors*
> *And do not lead us into temptation*
> *But deliver us from evil*
> *For Thine is the kingdom, and the power, and the glory forever*
> *Amen.*

While a study of every word of this prayer would be worth the time, we will focus on the line, *"Thy kingdom come, Thy will be done on earth as it is in heaven."*

Jesus told His disciples to prayer for the Father, who was in heaven, that His *"kingdom come"* (from heaven to earth).

COME: Erchomai (er'-khom-ahee)= to *come* or *go* (in a great variety of applications, literally and figuratively): - accompany, appear, bring, come enter, fall out, go, grow, X light, X next, pass, resort, be set.

They were on planet Earth, the terrestrial ball, the third rock from the sun, and they were able to pray and touch the heart of God, and His kingdom could come from heaven to earth which would in turn reflect His will. If their prayers could not touch and move God then Jesus was teaching them an exercise in futility. They were to pray with a expectancy that what they prayed would manifest not only in the *"sweet bye and bye"* but in the *"nitty gritty now and now."* I am finding out more and more as I live out my life on planet earth that the "sweet bye and bye" is really the "sweat bye and bye," because the struggle is real, and that is what makes it the "nitty gritty now and now."

KINGDOM: Basileia (bas-il-i'-ah)=From G935; properly *royalty*, that is, (abstractly) *rule*, or (concretely) a *realm* (literally or figuratively): - kingdom, + reign. G935: basileus (bas-il-yooce')=Probably from G939 (through the notion of a *foundation* of power); a *sovereign* (abstractly, relatively or figuratively): - king. G939: basis (bas'-ece)=From bainō (to *walk*); a *pace*, that is, (by implication) the *foot:* - foot.

The breakdown of this word kingdom means:
- Royalty
- Rule
- A realm
- Reign
- A foundation of power

- Sovereign
- Walk
- A pace
- The foot

So Jesus is telling His followers to pray for a *heavenly foundation of power* to *come from heaven* and be *established (rule and reign) on earth* which would reflect the Father's Kingdom will (wish, desire) as they walked on planet earth. Yes, this will eventually be fulfilled in His millennium Kingdom, but for now, until He returns, we can walk in His kingdom, now. This heavenly foundation will not be of a flesh and blood nature but a place where His *super* comes on our *natural.*

"The Kingdom of God is not meat or drink but righteousness, peace and joy in the Holy Ghost."

Romans 14:17

This Kingdom, this realm and foundation of power is based on:

RIGHTEOUSNESS: dikaiosunē (dik-ah-yos-oo'-nay)= From G1342; *equity* (of character or act); specifically (Christian) *justification:* - righteousness. G1342: dikaios dik'-ah-yos)= From G1349; *equitable* (in character or act); by implication *innocent, holy* (absolutely or relatively): - just, meet, right (-eous). G1349: dikē (dee'-kay)= *right* (as self *evident*), that is, *justice* (the principle, a decision, or its execution): - judgment, punish, vengeance.

This righteousness is not based on our own qualities or abilities but everything the Father is and always will be in us.

24

Anything that we can bring to the table falls under self-righteousness, but as we bring it to Him in obedience then God takes that and fleshes it out for us. God's righteousness is the standard by which all righteousness is measure. In the tent world the center post is called *the standard* by which all guide lines are attached to insure stability of the tent. So it is with everything we are and do. We are attached to the standard.

PEACE: eirēnē (i-rah'-nay)=Probably from a primary verb eirō (to *join*); *peace* (literally or figuratively); by implication *prosperity:* - one, peace, quietness, rest, + set at one again.

This peace is not a peace that is man-made. It is not even the absence of conflict, but is a peace that passes all understanding and comprehension (Philippians 4:7). It is a peace that takes crumbling man-made kingdoms and sets it at one again.

JOY: chara (khar-ah')=From G5463; *cheerfulness*, that is, calm *delight:* - gladness, X greatly, (X be exceeding) joy (-ful, -fully, -fulness, -ous). G5463: chairō (khah'ee-ro)=A primary verb; to be full of *cheer*, that is, calmly *happy* or well off; impersonal especially as a salutation (on meeting or parting), *be well:* - farewell, be glad, God speed, greeting, hail, joy (-fully), rejoice.

This joy is *not* some kind of emotional roller coaster based on current events and giddiness. Three of the definitions jumps out at me:
- cheerfulness
- calm delight
- calmly happy or well off

IN THE HOLY GHOST

All three of these aspects of the Kingdom of God including (1) righteousness, (2) peace, (3) joy are not found on a human level but on a spiritual level. That is why this Kingdom must be prayed down on a spiritual level. The character of the Kingdom on earth as it is in heaven can only be in the Holy Ghost. The Holy Ghost is not some kind of a cosmic force or even some kind of disjointed spirit floating around and haunting people, but a person of the God-head. More will be discussed about the Holy Ghost in chapters about the anointing and His presence in respect to power. Recommended Reading about the Holy Ghost includes:

- *The Presence and Work of the Holy Spirit* by R.A. Torrey
- *The Most Important Person On Earth: The Holy Spirit* by Myles Monroe
- *Charisma's Bible Handbook On The Holy Spirit* by John Rea
- *Come and Live* by Tom C. McKenney
- *Simple and Profound* by David du Plessis
- *The Gift of the Holy Spirit Today* by J. Rodman Williams

These are just a few works that would be worth your while on the subject of the Holy Ghost. If you really desire to read these books you may have to search them out. We will be looking at the Holy Ghost in other chapters.

HOMEWORK

1. Who did Jesus tell us that we are we to not to be like when we pray? (Matthew 6:5)
2. Why were the hypocrites praying as the stood in the synagogues and on the street corners? (Matthew 6:5)

NOTE: This does not mean that you can't pray in public, just be aware of why you are doing it.

3. What had the hypocrite received in full with their prayer attitudes? (Matthew 6:5)
4. In contrast to hypocrite prayers, what should be our prayer habit? (Matthew 6:6)
5. As you go to your inner room and close the door, who do you pray to? (Matthew 6:6)

NOTE: "Jewish tradition said that there was in the Temple, a "chamber of secrets" into which the devout used to put their gifts in secret so that the poor could receive support there from in secret." (Ryrie Bible Study notes on Matthew 6:4)

6. Where is your Father? (Matthew 6:6)
7. What will the Father, who is in secret, who sees what is done in secret, do for you? (Matthew 6:6)

NOTE: In I Corinthians 3:16 and I Corinthians 6:19 we see that our bodies are "the temple of the Holy Spirit" and that the Spirit of God dwells within us. The temple is from the Greek word, naos.

TEMPLE: naos (*nah-os'*)= (to *dwell*); a *fane, shrine, temple*: - shrine, temple. Compare G2411. 2411: hieron (*hee-er-on'*)= a *sacred* place, that is, the entire precincts (whereas G3485 denotes the central *sanctuary* itself) of the *Temple* (at Jerusalem or elsewhere): - temple.

NOTE: The actual physical temple had the main structure and deep within an inner room, a secret room. We are the "temple of God" which speaks of the inner place where God dwells in our human spirit. This is the true place of prayer versus outside, public places where we can get prideful in our prayers. Again, this does not mean we can't pray in public, but our attitude must be correct and not prideful like the hypocrite.

8. What are we not to use like the Gentiles use in prayer? (Matthew 6:7)

9. What do the Gentiles suppose? (Matthew 6:7)

10. What does the Father know when you pray? (Matthew 6:8)

NOTE: The Father know what we need before we ask, but Jesus still instructs us to ask in the Lord's prayer found in Matthew 6:9-15.

11. What did Jesus instruct the disciples to ask for concerning the kingdom in their prayers? (Matthew 6:10)

"Your kingdom, your rule, your reign, your foundation of power, your righteousness, your peace, your joy, your Holy Spirit, come..."

Matthew 6:9
with emphasis and addition mine

In our next chapter we will see how this Kingdom coming will be manifest on earth as it is in heaven.

CHAPTER THREE

THY WILL BE DONE

I n Chapter Two we established that there is a Kingdom, and the King in the Kingdom is God *our Father who art in heaven.* (Matthew 6:10) We also established in Chapter Two that this Kingdom is a rule (where there is a ruler), a realm (a real place), and is a foundation of power (authority and dynamic ability) based on righteousness, peace, and joy in the Holy Ghost. (Romans 14:17) Now, we will look at *the will of the King that will done on earth as it is in heaven.*

WILL: thelēma (thel'-ay-mah)=From the prolonged form of G2309; a *determination* (properly the thing), that is, (actively) *choice* (specifically *purpose, decree*; abstractly *volition*) or (passively) *inclination:* - desire, pleasure, will. G2309: thelō thethelō (thel'-o, eth-el'-o=Either the first or the second form may be used. In certain tenses theleō *thel-eh'-o* (and etheleō *eth-el-eh'-o*) are used, which are otherwise obsolete; apparently strengthened from the alternate form of G138; to *determine* (as an active voice *option* from subjective impulse; whereas G1014 properly denotes rather a passive voice *acquiescence* in objective considerations), that is, *choose* or *prefer* (literally or figuratively); by implication to *wish*, that is, *be inclined* to (sometimes adverbially *gladly*); impersonally for

29

the future tense, to *be about to*; by Hebraism to *delight in:* - desire, be disposed (forward), intend, list, love, mean, please, have rather, (be) will (have, -ling, -ling [ly]).

As we extract the meanings from the definition we get the idea that His will *on earth* is something that He truly *desires* for those who are praying for His Kingdom and His will, *as it is in heaven*. His will means:

- Determination
- Choice
- Purpose
- Volition
- Inclination
- Pleasure
- Desire
- Preference
- Wish
- To be about

Lately I have been praying Matthew 6:10 with a new perspective. Of course we pray for the eventual coming of His millennium Kingdom and will to be manifested when there will be a new heaven and a new earth (Revelation 21:1), but also for *here and now* in this nitty-gritty world that we live (regulate and conduct) our lives by faith. (II Corinthians 5:7)

"For we walk by faith [we regulate our lives and conduct ourselves by our conviction or belief respecting man's relationship to God and divine things with trust and holy fervor; thus we walk] not by sight or appearance."

2 Corinthians 5:7, AMP

"Then I saw a new heaven and a new earth; for the first heaven and the first earth passed away, and there is no longer any sea."

Revelation 21:1

Now, lately, I have been praying:

"Thy righteousness, peace and joy in the Holy Ghost come, Thy determination, choice, purpose, volition, inclination, pleasure, desire, preference, wish to be done and about what you want on earth (where we live) as it is in heaven (where You live)."

Matthew 6:10
with additions mine

I also am praying it like this:

"Thy Kingdom rule, reign and foundation of power come, Thy healing be done (accomplished), on earth (where sickness is) AS IT IS in heaven (where there is no sickness)."

Matthew 6:10
with emphasis and addition mine

When you read the gospels of Matthew, Mark, Luke and John you see Jesus ministering for a three year period. When Jesus was baptized by John in the Jordan River it was the beginning of His ministry after He came out of the waters and the Spirit of God came down upon Him and He received affirmation of pleasure from the Father. (Matthew 3:13-17) He was immediately led by the Spirit throughout the wilderness and was tempted by the d-evil and came out the other side of the wilderness temptation experience full of the Spirit. (Matthew 4:1-11; Luke 4:1-14) It is at this point that Jesus began to go about under the anointing of the Holy Spirit and power.

> *"And you know of Jesus of Nazareth how God anointed Him with the Holy Ghost and power and how He went about doing good, and healing all who were oppressed by the d-evil for God was with Him."*
>
> Acts 10:38

> *"And you know of Jesus (The Healer) of Nazareth (local boy) how God (The Anointer) anointed (poured out) Him (Jesus the Healer) with the Holy Ghost and power (duNAmis, dynamic ability) and how He (Jesus the Healer) went about doing good (not bad) and healing (the will of God) ALL who were harassed and oppressed by the d-evil (not God) for God was with Him (Jesus the Healer) for God was with Him (with the anointing, Immanuel God with us)."*
>
> Acts 10:38
> with emphasis and addition mine

This going about doing good and healing was the *expression and demonstrated* the Kingdom of God and the will of God on earth as it was and is in heaven. Jesus came for the purpose of *destroying the works of the d-evil.* (I John 3:8)

You cannot separate the Kingdom of God coming from His will being done on earth as it is in heaven. We have previously defined the will (thelema) of God but we now look at it compared to His will (boulema). First we refresh our memories with *"thelema"* and then look at *"bouloma"*

WILL: thelēma (thel'-ay-mah)=From the prolonged form of G2309; a *determination* (properly the thing), that is, (actively) *choice* (specifically *purpose, decree*; abstractly *volition*) or (passively) *inclination:* - desire, pleasure, will.

> *"Thy Kingdom come Thy will (thelema) be done on earth as it is in heaven."*
>
> Matthew 6:10

This determination, choice, purpose, decree, volition, inclination, desire and pleasure is what Jesus taught us to pray to be done on planet Earth as it is in heaven. We are to pray for this rule and realm and the desire of the King to be manifested. Of course, this will is not always manifested because of either unbelief/lack of faith, or choosing to do the opposite thing. The will (boulema) of God is that none should perish but that all have everlasting life, but this is not always the case secondary to choices made.

WILL: Boulomai (boo'-lom-ahee)=Middle voice of a primary verb; to *will*, that is, (reflexively) *be willing:* - be disposed, minded, intend, list (be, of own) will (-ing).

> *"The Lord is not slack concerning his promise, as some men count slackness; but is longsuffering to us-ward, not willing (boulema) that any should perish, but that all should come to repentance."*
>
> II Peter 3:9

33

Bob Mumford, in his book *The King and You* explains the differences between the two wills (thelema and boulema) like this:

"We need to understand that there are two different words used in the Greek for our English word will, as it is used throughout Scripture. One is boulema, the other is thelema. Boulema means the eternal counsels of God which are unfolding through the ages—His purpose—His determination. It is going to be done whether you and I like it or not. God's intention will come to pass. However, thelema, which means God's wish or desire, *most often* depends upon the response of the individual for fulfillment." (Bob Mumford)

This thing called, "the will of God", whether it is "thelema" or "boulomai" is like a coin with inscriptions on both side. Like a quarter there is one side with George Washington engraved and on the other side an eagle is engraved. Both sides are significant but separate with the two sides forming one coin. It speaks to me of the sovereignty of God with God being God doing anything that He wants but leaves His will as a choice on our part.

In our next chapter we will look at how faith plays apart in this will of God can be revealed on earth as it is in heaven. Can it be possible that human beings can possibly have a part in ushering in the will of God in to our everyday situations and circumstances? The answer is a resounding YES!

HOMEWORK

1. What did Jesus tell us to pray to come? (Matthew 6:10)
2. In connection with the rule, reign, foundation of power (the Kingdom) coming, what was to be done? (Matthew 6:10)

3. Where was this Kingdom will to be done? (Matthew 6:10)
4. Where was the template for this Kingdom will? (Matthew 6:10)

NOTE: I look at the Kingdom in heaven to be headquarters of the Father and His kingdom manifested on earth is the outpost where we colonize and demonstrate His will. I will look up to heaven and see if I can find sickness, sin, disease, dis-comfort, dys-function. I then pray for whatever is in heaven to be manifested here on earth.

Chapter Four

ON EARTH (PRE-FALL)

We have mentioned that one of the verses that are the basis for this book is Matthew 6:10. A part of that verse is the phrase, "…on earth as it is in heaven." This speaks of two locations where one is not of this world (heaven) while the other is of the world where we live (earth).

In this chapter we will look at the earth at the point of "in the beginning" as we look at the genesis of this world where we currently reside. We will look at earth before the fall, before the curse, before death was set into motion, both spiritual and physical.

We will look at the roots of a world before a lie was believed. In the following chapter (chapter five) we will look at on earth (post fall) where there is sin, sickness, dis-ease, dis-order, and dis-function all under the oppression by the d-evil.

The book of Genesis is a book of beginnings of many things. The word genesis means "creation" or "generation and/or beginnings,"

BEGINNING: (ray-sheeth'*)*= the *first*, in place, time, order or rank (specifically a *firstfruit*): - beginning, chief (-est), first (-fruits, part, time), principal thing.

"In the beginning (genesis) God created (prepared, formed, fashioned) the heavens and the earth."

Genesis 1:1, AMP
with additions mine

God pulls the curtain back to the creative process and gives us a glimpse of His wonderful imagination and how he brought to pass His desires, His will with planet earth and the inhabitants. God had a thought, spoke out His thoughts and it was so.

"Then God said, 'Let (allow) there be light; and there was light.'"

Genesis 1:1
with addition mine

In the creative processes (Genesis 1:1-Genesis 2:1-25) God:
- Created
- Said
- Saw
- Separated
- Called
- Made
- Placed
- Blessed
- Gave authority
- Gave
- Rested
- Formed
- Panted
- Placed

- Took
- Placed
- Caused
- Fashioned/Built

Throughout this seven day period of creation God underscored His approval at least (according to my count) seven times that His creation was *good* and not only was it *good* but it was *"very good."*

In Genesis 1:1-31 we see the creative process through a telescopic view and then starting with Genesis 2:1-25 we see the creative process through a microscopic view. I always think about many of the firsts that took place in this book of beginnings.

- First CPR (Cardio-Pulmonary Resuscitation) as God formed man from dust of the ground, and breathed His breath of life into his nostrils with the cause and effect being man became a living being/soul. (Genesis 2:7)
- First planted Garden (Genesis 2:8)
- First crop/harvest for food. (Genesis 2:9)
- First establishment of the tree of the knowledge of good and evil. (Genesis 2:10)
- First rivers flowing out of the Garden of Eden. (Genesis 2:10-11)
- First mention of gold and jewels (precious stones). (Genesis 2:11-12)
- First job description for man as a gardener (to cultivate and keep the garden). (Genesis 2:16)
- First commandments and restrictions for man (eat freely from any tree except from the tree of knowledge of good and evil). (Genesis 2:16-17)
- First mention of death (the day that you eat (in

disobedience) you shall surely die. (Genesis 2:17)

- First mention of need of a helper (helpmeet) to keep man from being alone (Genesis 2:18) **NOTE**: In Genesis 1:26 we see that God created man in His/Our image and likeness and described this man as them (male and female) and gave them both authority over all creation on earth. (Genesis 1:26-31) In the microscopic view of Genesis 2 we see a close up look of the progression of the creation of man (male) first and then the wo-man (female) (Genesis 2:18) **NOTE TO THE NOTE**: This fact is important when we look at the fall when the serpent creeps into the garden, as man (male/ Adam and female/Eve were both given authority over everything that creeps (moves) on the earth. God gave authority over the creep and we also have authority over the creep because of Jesus. (Genesis 1:30)
- First mention of man giving name to the animals. (Genesis 2:19-20) As Adam is giving names to the animals not one of them was suitable to be a helper to him. (Genesis 2:20)
- First anesthesiology as God caused a deep sleep to fall upon man. (Genesis 2:21)
- First surgery (ribectomy) and the first surgical closure. (Genesis 2:21)
- First fashion show as God fashioned/built into a woman from the rib (Genesis 2:21)
- First wedding as the Father walked the bride down the aisle to the groom as God brought her to man. (Genesis 2:22)
- First wedding vows and pronouncement of man and wife. (Genesis 2:24)

HOMEWORK

1. Who was in the beginning? (Genesis 1:1)
2. What process did God initiate? (Genesis 1:1)
3. What did God create? (Genesis 1:1)
4. What were the three conditions of the earth? (Genesis 1:2)

NOTE: Some believe that earth had already been created and there was some kind of cataclysmic (relating to or denoting a violent natural event) event that took place to plunge earth into a formless, void, dark mess. Some believe that Genesis 1:1 was a re-creation versus initial creation. I have no clue (and really no one else does). All I know is that it is revealed to us that God changed chaos by the spoken word and it was His will to do so. I also like to apply Genesis 1:1 to II Corinthians 5:17 where God spoke to the chaos in me and made me a new creation.

5. Who was moving over the surface of the water on earth? (Genesis 1:2)

MOVED: râchaph (raw-khaf')=A primitive root; to *brood*; by implication to *be relaxed:* - flutter, move, shake.

NOTE: This movement of the Holy Spirit over the surface of the waters is like a mother hen brooding, sweeping fluttering her wings over her eggs or baby chicks.

6. What did God use in the creative process over the formless, void and darkness? (Genesis 1:3)

NOTE: God expressed His thoughts, His desire, His will via the spoken Word. I believe that this Word Spoken is Jesus. Jesus is called the Word and actually was God Himself (John 1:1-14) and is attributed to be the Creator (or at least in the creative process) (Colossians1:15-18) and also is attributed as the one whom the world was made. (Hebrews 1:2-4)

7. What word was used to declare thought about His creation? (Genesis 1:4, 10, 12, 18, 21, 25, 31)

NOTE: It appears that God had a conference up in heaven as He spoke forth His desire to create someone in *their* (plural) own image and likeness. (Genesis 1:26-27)

8. Who did God created in His own image? (Genesis 1:26-27)
9. What was man created in? (Genesis 1:27)
10. What were the two components of this creation called man? (Genesis 1:27)
11. What did God do for these two created beings? (Genesis 1:28)

BLESSED: bârak (baw-rak')=A primitive root; to *kneel*; by implication to *bless* God (as an act of adoration), and (vice-versa) man (as a benefit); also (by euphemism) to *curse* (God or the king, as treason): - X abundantly, X altogether, X at all, blaspheme, bless, congratulate, curse, X greatly, X indeed, kneel (down), praise, salute, X still, thank.

NOTE: Later we will see that these two creations (male and female) would become husband and wife.

12. What did God give man, both male and female? (Genesis 1:26)

RULE/DOMINION/AUTHORITY: râdâh (raw-daw')=A primitive root; to *tread* down, that is, *subjugate*; specifically to *crumble* off: - (come to, make to) have dominion, prevail against, reign, (bear, make to) rule, (-r, over), take.

NOTE: This dominion/rule was over many things but one thing that they had dominion/rule over was, "…over every creeping thing that creeps on the earth." (Genesis 1:26) I believe this would include the ultimate creep, the serpent (aka the d-evil, satan). In Genesis chapter 3 we will see that Adam and Eve (male and female, man and wo-man) did not use their dominion, rule and authority.

In the next chapter we will see the fall and the entrance of death, sickness, dis-ease, dis-comfort, and dys-function.

CHAPTER FIVE

ENTER THE SERPENT (THE FALL)
Genesis 3:1-24

T he title to this chapter is a nod to the Bruce Lee (martial artist) classic movie, *Enter The Dragon*.

> *"Now the serpent..."*
>
> Genesis 3:1

> *"Now the serpent was more subtle and crafty than any living creature of the field which the Lord God had made. And he [satan] said to the woman, 'can it really be that God has said, you shall not eat from every tree of the garden?"*
>
> Genesis 3:1, AMP

This unholy entity has been identified as a "creep" who the man and the woman had dominion, rule, and authority over. (Genesis 1:26, Genesis 3:1) We will see that A & E (Adam and Eve) did not utilize the authority with what they were blessed. So many believers who are in Christ do not utilize the authority (exousia, delegated authority) that they were given by Jesus. I believe that as Christians when we try to manifest power (duNAmis, dynamic ability) without walking in the delegated authority that we were given, then we will have the same results as A & E (Adam and Eve) in the garden.

This serpent has been identified by many personas including *the d-evil.* I like to spell devil like this, d-evil and then say he is de evil one. Also I refuse to capitalize his name because in my mind he does not deserve it. If you spell *d-evil* backwards it spells *live-d* which describes what happens when Jesus died on the cross, was buried and on the third day rose from the dead, we live-d as he reversed the curse. In the book of The Revelation of Jesus revealed to John on the island of Patmos, the many of the names of this serpent.

> *"And there was a war in heaven, Michael and his angels waging war with the dragon and the dragon and his angels waged war, and they were not strong enough, and there was no longer a place found for them in heaven. And the great dragon was thrown down, the serpent of old who is called the d-evil and satan, who deceives the whole world; he was thrown down to the earth, and his angels were thrown down with him. And I heard a loud voice in heaven saying, 'Now the salvation, and the power and the kingdom of our God and the authority of His Christ have come, for the accuser of our brethren has been thrown, who accuses them before our God day and night."*

Revelation 12:7-10

This serpent, dragon, d-evil, deceiver, liar, thief, stealer killer, destroyer, accuser of the brethren, tempter, that crept into the garden was an angelic being in charge of worship in heaven and led a rebellion against God and was cast out of heaven along with 1/3 of the angels. (See Luke 10:18, Isaiah 14:12-14, Ezekiel 28:14-18 for full details).

> *"And it is no wonder, for satan himself masquerades as an angel of light, so it is not surprising if his servants also masquerade as ministers of righteousness. [But] their end will correspond with their deeds."*
> II Corinthians 11:14-15, AMP
> with emphasis mine

THE STRUGGLE OF TEMPTATION

> *"For our struggle is not against flesh and blood, but against the rulers, against the powers against the world forces of this darkness, against the spiritual forces of wickedness in the heavenly places."*
> Ephesians 6:12

NOTE: The struggle is real.

Adam and Eve were flesh and blood but the serpent was not flesh and blood. If A & E (Adam and Eve) resisted on a spiritual level instead of a fleshly level, the outcome would have been very different.

> *"For we are not wrestling with flesh and blood [contending only with physical opponents], but against the powers, against [the master spirits who are] the world rulers of this present darkness, against the spirit forces of wickedness in the heavenly (supernatural) sphere."*
> Ephesians 6:10, AMP
> with addition mine

The serpent, the d-evil has well-orchestrated schemes against us backed up with his angelic followers in the form of:
- Rulers
- The Powers
- The World Forces of this (present) darkness
- Spiritual Forces of wickedness

These schemes take place not on earth (where there is flesh and blood) but in the heavenly places. We are called (and so is Adam and Eve) to:
- Be strong in the Lord
- Be strong in the strength of the Lord
- Resist the d-evil in the evil day
- Stand firm after having done everything

THE TEMPTATION

"Temptation is not necessarily designed to pull you *into* something as much as it is designed to pull you *away* from who you really are." (Larry Napier teaching at Belmont Church in the 70's on spiritual warfare) This type of temptation happened to Adam and Eve, Jesus, the disciples/apostles and us. Temptation happens with the lust of the eyes, the lust of the flesh and the boastful pride of life in this world. (I John 2:15-17)

The serpent tempted Eve on three different levels:
1. Indeed has God said, you shall not eat from any tree of the garden? The d-evil planted doubt in the garden of Eve's mind about what God said.

"And the Lord God commanded the man, saying, 'from any tree of the garden you may eat freely; but (in contrast to eating freely) from the tree of the knowledge of good and

evil you surely shall not eat for in the day that you eat from it you shall surely die."

Genesis 2:16-17

Eve demonstrated that she knew what God had said but she did add something to what God said.

"And the woman said to the serpent, 'from the fruit of the tree which is in the middle of the garden, God has said, 'you shall not eat from it or touch it, lest you die."

Genesis 3:2-3

Looking at Genesis 2:16-17 we see that God did say "you shall not eat" but God did not say, "or touch it". While this may seem nit-picky God did not say, "or touch it". Of course to eat that forbidden fruit you would have to touch it like bobbing for apples, you can't touch with your hands but you will touch with your teeth, lips and tongue. The bottom line is Eve knew the limitations and chose to disobey.

NOTE: I have heard it said over the years by various people (who I can't remember now) that this disobedience was on the same level as high treason in governments. Obedience is not supposed to be a hardship. When we resist God's will, *oBEDience* (a place of rest) becomes *oBEATience* (a place of struggle).

"He who has My (commandments) and keeps them, he it is who loves me and he who loves Me will be loved by My Father and I will love him and will disclose, reveal, manifest"

John 14:21
with addition mine

NOTE: If you want a disclosure, a revelation, a manifestation of Jesus in our lives, it is hinged on our love for Him and *oBEDience* to Him.

NOTE: Nowhere does it say in the Bible that the "forbidden fruit" was an "apple". Some have speculated that the lump in the throat of man, called the "Adams's Apple" happened as the "apple" that Adam took from Eve hung in his throat and thus the name. I personally believe that the fruit was the pomegranate that is the cursed fruit with all of its seeds. Hey, if everyone else can speculate, why can't I?

2. And the serpent said to the woman, 'you *surely shall not die!*'" (Genesis 3:5)

Once again, the d-evil tries to place doubt in the mind of Eve about the cause and effect of disobedience. How many of us do something that we know that is wrong by not believing that there will be consequences to our actions as we disobey what God plainly stated?

"…you shall *surely die.*" (Genesis 2:17)

Once again, the serpent tries to twist what Jesus said.

3. For God knows that in the day you eat from it *your eyes will be opened* and *you will be like God*, knowing good and evil."

Now we get to the root of the problem, the d-evil wants to be like God, exalted above God to receive the worship that is due to God. The serpent tries to turn it around that God wants to withhold the honor from Eve. With these three twisted truths (which are really lies) the woman was faced with a choice of her free will and she choose unwisely based on the lust of the flesh, the lust of the eyes, and the boastful pride of life.

"When the woman saw that the tree was good for food, and that it was a delight to the eyes, and that the tree was desirable to make one wise, she took from its fruit and ate; and she gave also to her husband with her, and he ate."

(Genesis 3:6)

NOTE: I have heard people (usually men) put all the blame on the wo-man but God originally gave the command to the man (Adam) before the woman was created. In the grand scheme of God's creation of man and woman, both were made in His image and likeness and both were given authority over the creeps and both were given the commandments along with the free will to choose and obey or ignore and disobey. (Genesis 1:26-30) Their choices ushered in death, dying, and the curse in this world.

This act of what has been described by some as "high treason", this act of disobedience and the effects of the cause was not limited to just two people in a garden but spread down through the ages, world-wide to every society, every social economic strata, to every religion, race, creed, color of the current 7 billion + (give or take a billion) on planet earth, terra firma, the blue planet, the third rock from the sun.

"As it is written, there is none righteous, no not one."
Romans 3:10

"For all have sinned and fall short of the glory of God."
Romans 3:23

"All of us like sheep have gone astray, each of us has turned

49

to his own way; but the Lord has caused the iniquity of us all to fall on Him."

Isaiah 53:6

"Therefore, just as through one man (Adam) sin entered into the world, and death through sin, and so death spread to all men, because all have sinned."

Romans 5:12

ENTER DEATH, DYING, SICKNESS, HARDSHIP AND THE CURSE

This thing that God created and declared that it was not only good but that it was *very good*, (Genesis 1:31) now has taken a turn for the worse.

God had told Adam and Even (man/male and wo-man/fe-male) that, "in the day that you eat from it you shall surely *die.*" (Genesis 2:17) It is note-worthy that A & E (Adam and Eve) did not keel over the moment that they took a bite of disobedience. So either God lied or was mistaken about the timing of this thing called *death*. I don't think so. The death of separation from the presence of the Lord had begun and the eventual physical death would follow.

"Then the eyes of both of them were opened, and they knew that they were naked; and they sewed fig leaves together and made themselves loin coverings. And they heard the sound of the Lord God walking in the garden in the cool of the day, and the man and his wife hid themselves from the presence of the Lord God among the trees of the garden."

Genesis 3:7-8

Self-imposed separation from God was the first sign of the death process. Hiding themselves among creation thinking they were hidden from God is a common mistake we make today.

NOTE: So often when we sin, we try to separate ourselves from God and other Christians.

THE BLAME GAME

"Then the Lord God called to the man, and said to him, 'where are you?"

Genesis 3:9

Adam's response was, "I heard the sound of Thee in the garden, and I was afraid because I was naked; so I hid myself."

Adam and Eve hid themselves from the very thing that could bring the refreshing from the fear and shame, the presence of the Lord.

"So repent (change your mind and purpose); turn around and return [to God], that your sins may be erased (blotted out, wiped clean), that times of refreshing) of recovering from the effects of heat, of reviving with fresh air) may come from the presence of the Lord."

Acts 3:19, AMP
with addition mine

Here is the dialogue between the Creator and the created.

God: Where are you?

Adam: I heard the sound of Thee in the garden, and *I was afraid* because I was naked; so I hid myself

God: Who told you that you were naked? Have you eaten from the tree of which I commanded you not to eat?

Adam: (let the blame game begin), *the woman* whom Thou gave to be with me, she gave from the tree, and I ate.

NOTE: Adam did the two-fold blame (1*) He blamed God* for giving him the wo-man (2) *He blamed the wo-man* for giving him the fruit. He finally confessed that, "I ate."

God to the woman (Eve): What is this you have done?

Eve*: The serpent* deceived me, and I ate.

God to the serpent: Because you have done this, *cursed* are you more than all cattle, and more than every beast of the field. And on your belly shall you go, and the dust shall you eat all the days of your life. I will put enmity between you and the woman, and between your seed and her seed; He shall bruise you on the head, and you shall bruise him on the heel.

NOTE: Genesis 3:15 is looked as a Messianic prophetic passage about the death of Jesus and the victory of Jesus over the serpent with His death, burial, and resurrection.

"And the God of peace will soon crush satan under your feet."

Romans 16:20

God to the woman: I will greatly multiply your pain in childbirth, in pain you shall bring forth children, yet your desire shall be for your husband and he shall rule over you.

God to Adam: *Because you have listened to the voice of your wife* and have eaten from the tree about which I commanded you, saying, you shall not eat from it, cursed is the ground because of you, in toil you shall eat of it all the days of your life. Both thorns and thistles it shall grow for you, and you shall eat the plants of the field, by the sweat of your face/brow you shall eat bread, till you return to the ground, because rom it you were taken, for you are dust, and to dust you shall return.

GOD'S PROVISION IN THE CURSE

The Lord God made garments of skin (first animal sacrifice). The animals did not have zippers on their hides *so blood had to be shed* to provide a covering for their shame. Then God drove them out of the garden and set a guard at the entrance to the garden to keep man away from the tree of life and they eat and live forever in the curse.

NOTE: This is the first mention of a chauffeur in the Bible where *God drove them out* of the garden. (Genesis 3:24) This goes along with *the first mention of a car* in the New Testament where the disciples were, *"all in one accord."* (Acts 2:1)

God has *provided His provision* in curse with Jesus the Christ. He uses blood to deal with the death, dying and curse but this time it was not the blood of bulls and goats which was temporary but the blood of Jesus for healing.

"For it is impossible for the blood of bulls and goats to take away sins."

Hebrews 10:12

"Surely our griefs (sickness) He Himself bore, and our sorrows (pains) He carried; yet we ourselves esteemed Him stricken, smitten of God, and afflicted. But He was pierced (wounded) through for our transgressions, He was crushed for our iniquities; the chastening for our well-being (peace)

fell up Him, and by His scourging (stripes we are healed)."
Isaiah 53:4, Matthew 8:17, I Peter 2:24-25
with addition mine

So there you have where mankind fell from, the cause and effect in our lives because of the high treason of disobedience, and the price paid for healing. The d-evil tries to convince us that we are still under the curse and that the will of God for us is to be sick. We don't deny reality (that we live in a cursed and fallen world) but we do deny reality's right to rule our lives. The will of God is healing.

HOMEWORK

1. Who was considered to be craftier than any beast of the field? (Genesis 3.1)
2. Who spoke first, the woman or the serpent? (Genesis 3:1)
3. What was the first question that the serpent posed to the woman? (Genesis 3:2)

NOTE: The thing the serpent used on the woman is the thing that he uses on us, doubt.

4. What was the response of the woman to the serpent? (Genesis 3:2-3)
5. God had told A & E (Adam and Eve) they *would* die. (Genesis 2:17) What did the serpent say would not happen? (Genesis 2:4)
6. What did the serpent tell the woman about God's motives? (Genesis 3:5)

NOTE: The serpent tries to characterize God as holding out on A & E.

7. What three things did the woman see as she believed

the serpent's lies? (Genesis 3:6)

8. What two things did Eve do? (Genesis 3:6)
9. What was the cause and effect of Adam and Eve disobeying God? (Genesis 3:7)
10. What was Adam's and Eve's response to God after they were disobedient to His Word? (Genesis 3:9-10)
11. When God quizzed Adam who tow people did he blame? (Genesis 3:11-12)
12. When God turned His attention to Eve and quizzed her, who did she blame? (Genesis 3:13)

NOTE: At this time, God spoke forth the curse to the serpent, the woman and the man. (Genesis 3:14-19)

MESSIANIC PROPHECY CONCERNING THE DEATH OF JESUS

"And I will put (God) will put enmity between you (the serpent) and the woman, and between your (the serpent) seed and her seed, and He (Jesus) shall bruise you on the head and you (the serpent) shall bruise him on the heel."

Genesis 3:15
with addition mine

NOTE: From Genesis to the Gospels we see the serpent/ the d-evil attempting to stop Genesis 3:15 from taking place, but he failed. Jesus was mocked, bruised, tortured, and nailed to a cross where He died but the serpent's head was bruised when on the 3rd day Jesus rose from the dead.

In our next chapter we will take a look about what happened on the cross of the Suffering Messiah for our sins and our sickness.

CHAPTER SIX

BY HIS STRIPES WE WERE HEALED

Isaiah 53 is a Messianic prophecy concerning the passion of Jesus on the cross as the Suffering Messiah. The controversy over the years by many theologians and Christians is what does "…by His stripes we are healed" mean?

In one camp you have those who believe that it speaks *only* of "sin sickness" because after all, that is why Jesus came to planet earth, to die in our place so we can have forgiveness of our sins. The bloody death, the burial of the stone cold dead body of Jesus and His glorious resurrection from the dead is why He came and that is *only reason* for why He came. On the surface, who can argue with that logic. If you do you are branded a heretic or at the least ignorant, deluded, and/or a fool.

In the other camp you have those who believe that "by His stripes we are healed" speaks of *not only* sin sickness but also of physical sickness. Back in the 40's 50's 60's and beyond to 2018 there are people who are proponents of healing being the will of God on earth as it is in heaven. These include but are not limited to Pentecostals, healing evangelists, charismatics and organizations like The Full Gospel Businessmen International (F.G.B.I.)

Whatever side you camp on, the bottom line is it definitely is a picture of Jesus and His work on the cross.

"Surely He has borne our griefs-sickness, weakness and distress- and carried our sorrows and pain [of punishment]. Yet we ignorantly considered Him stricken and afflicted by God [as if with leprosy]. But (in contrast) He was wounded for our transgressions, He was bruised for our guilt and iniquities; the chastisement needful to obtain peace and well-being for us was upon Him, and with the stripes that wounded Him and we are healed and made whole.

Isaiah 53:4-5, AMP
with additions mine

HOMEWORK

1. Who has believed our message? (Isaiah 53:1, John 12:38, Romans 10:16)

NOTE: The message is about the Suffering Messiah on the Cross. Watchman Nee (Chinese Believer who as martyred) and wrote many books including The Normal Christian Life, states that when he mentions the cross that he is speaking of the Death, the Burial and the Resurrection of Jesus.

2. According to John (the beloved disciple) what was the message they heard from Him and announce to us? (I John 1:5)
3. What is not in Him? (I John 1:5)
4. How did (Jesus) grow up before Him (the Father)? (Isaiah 53:2)
5. What did He not have? (Isaiah 53:2)
6. Did He have an appearance that we should be attracted to Him? (Isaiah 53:2)
7. Who despised and forsook Him? (Isaiah 53:3)
8. What was He acquainted with? (Isaiah 53:3)

9. What would men hide? (Isaiah 53:3)

10. He was despised. What did we not do? (Isaiah 53:3)

NOTE: The next few questions and answers will be gleaned from quote from the Amplified Bible.

> "*Surely He has borne our griefs-sickness, weakness and distress- and carried our sorrows and pain [of punishment]. Yet we ignorantly considered Him stricken and afflicted by God [as if with leprosy]. But (in contrast) He was wounded for our transgressions, He was bruised for our guilt and iniquities; the chastisement needful to obtain peace and well-being for us was upon Him, and with the stripes that wounded Him and we are healed and made whole.*
>
> Isaiah 53:4-5, AMP
> with addition mine

11. What has He borne? (Isaiah 53:4, AMP)
   •
   •
   •
   •

12. What did He carry? (Isaiah 53:4, AMP)

13. What did we ignorantly consider concerning Him and God? (Isaiah 53:4, AMP)
   •
   •

14. What physical attribute was considered about Him being stricken and afflicted? (Isaiah 53:4, AMP)

NOTE: I find it interesting that people considered mistakenly that Jesus was stricken and afflicted by God. Today, we still are mistaken that sickness and disease stricken us and afflicts us is by God. Sickness is harassment and oppression by the d-evil.

15. Why was Jesus wounded? (Isaiah 53:5, AMP))

TRANSGRESSION: peh'-shah = a revolt (national, moral or religious): - rebellion, sin, transgression, trespassive

NOTE: Transgressions means to *"go beyond known limits"*. It is like we know the Law posted on the roads, to go a certain amount of speed, but we choose to go "beyond known limits".

16. Why was He bruised? (Isaiah 53:5, AMP)
•
•

17. Why was the chastisement upon Him? (Isaiah 53:5, AMP)

18. What was the purpose of the stripes that wounded Him? (Isaiah 53:5, AMP)
•
•

HEALED: râphâ' râphâh (raw-faw', raw-faw')=A primitive root; properly to mend (by stitching), that is, (figuratively) to cure: - cure, (cause to) heal, physician, repair, X thoroughly, make whole. H7503:râphâh (raw-faw')=A primitive root; to slacken (in many applications, literally or figuratively): - abate, cease, consume, draw [toward evening], fail, (be) faint, be (wax) feeble, forsake, idle, leave, let alone (go, down), (be) slack, stay, be still, be slothful, (be) weak (-en). H7495.râphâ' râphâh (raw-faw', raw-faw')=A primitive root; properly to mend (by stitching), that is, (figuratively) to cure: - cure, (cause to) heal, physician, repair, X thoroughly, make whole.

NOTE: Now let's take a look at the New Testament meaning of Isaiah 53:4.

19. Whose home did Jesus enter in Capernaum? (Matthew 8:1614, Mark 1:29, Luke 4:38)

20. What was the condition of Peter's mother-in-law? (Matthew 8:14, Mark 1:30, Luke 4:38)

21. What did Jesus do? (Matthew 8:14, Mark 1:31, Luke 4:39)

NOTE: Jesus touched her hand, raised her up by her hand and stood her up and rebuked the fever. This fever was not from God. if it was then Jesus was rebuking the work of His Father. Jesus only said what the Father said and did what the Father did. (John 5:19, John 8:28, John 12:47)

22. What was the cause and effect of the touch, the raising up into a standing position and speaking/rebuking the mountain of fever? (Matthew 8:15, Mark 1:31, Luke 4:39, Mark 11:20-26)

NOTE: Word gets around about Jesus healing Peter's mother-in-law from the harassment and oppression by the d-evil (Acts 10:38)

23. Who were people bringing to Jesus? (Matthew 8:16, Mark 1:32-33, Luke 4:40)

NOTE: The problem with the people brought to Jesus was:
- demon possessed
- sick
- various diseases.

24. What did Jesus do to those who were brought to Him at Peter's house? (Matthew 8:16, Mark 1:34, Luke 4:40)

25. How many did Jesus heal? (Matthew 8:16)

26. What was fulfilled when Jesus healed ALL who was sick? (Isaiah 53:4, Matthew 8:17, I Peter 2:24-25)

NOTE: Jesus went on for 3 years doing this healing. *If* Isaiah 53:4-5 was fulfilled with the healing then it would hold true for healing of sin sickness on the same cross.

In our next chapter we will look at the M.O. of Jesus status post anointing with the Holy Spirit after His water baptism.

CHAPTER SEVEN

THE HEALER'S MODUS OPERANDI (M.O.)

The Healer (Jesus) came from heaven down to earth in the form of a baby, grew up of 30 years and then for the final three years of His earthly life, demonstrated the Kingdom Will of God on earth AS IT IS in heaven. Then He was crucified and died, was buried, and rose from the dead (aka Death, Burial, Resurrection of Jesus the Christ).

Today we look at the Modus Operandi of The Healer.

Jesus made His first appearance on planet Earth as a baby in Bethlehem. His appearance was first mentioned in Genesis 3:15 as a Messianic prophecy of His death and the bruising of the serpent's head. As mentioned in a previous chapter from first mention in the Old Testament all the way to and through the Gospels in the New Testament, we see the serpent trying everything he could do to stop the bruising of his head.

Jesus knew at least three things found in John 13:3.

a. The Father had given all things into His hands

b. That He had come forth from God

c. He was going back to God

For three years on planet earth Jesus demonstrated the will of God on earth as it is in heaven (Matthew 6:10)

Jesus had a purpose.

"The Son of God appeared for this purpose, to destroy the works of the d-evil"

I John 3:8

Jesus spoke of this purpose and how He would be anointed by Spirit of God coming on Him. This was a prophecy from Isaiah 61:1-2 and was manifested in the Gospels and underscored in Acts 10:38 and Luke 4:18-19.

a. He would go about doing good and healing all who were oppressed by the d-evil.

b. He would preach the Good News (aka The Gospel) to the poor.

c. He was sent to proclaim release to the captive (as well as release the captives from the harassment and oppression of the d-evil.

d. He was sent to proclaim the recovery of the sight to the blind (physical and spiritual blindness)

e. He was sent to free those who are oppressed.

f. He was sent to proclaim/declare the favorable year of the Lord.

Jesus' Modus Operandi (M.O.) for three years is found in Matthew 4:23). The cause and effect of Jesus being obedient in His purpose is found in Matthew 4:24

a. Jesus was going throughout all Galilee.

b. Jesus was teaching in their synagogues.

c. Jesus was proclaiming/declaring the gospel (good news) of the Kingdom.

d. Jesus was healing (the will of God on earth as it is in heaven) every kind of sickness among the people.

The cause and effect of Jesus' Modus Operandi was found in Matthew 4:24.

a. The news about Him spread throughout all Syria.

b. They brought to Him all who were ill, suffering with various diseases and pains, demoniacs, epileptics, paralytics; and He healed them.

c. Large crowds followed Him from Galilee and the Decapolis and Jerusalem and Judea, and from beyond the Jordan.

When Jesus was preparing for the Cross (the Death, Burial, Resurrection) He told His followers that He was going back to the Father and that He would sent back "another" comforter (one of the same kind as He was, John 14:16)) and that they would carry on His purpose by doing the same works and even greater works. (John 14:12-14) He would ask the Father to send the Holy Spirit, the Helper to help them do these things. (John 14:16)

Jesus later would expand those who would do what He taught them (the 12) in Matthew 28:18-20, John 17:20. That means from then until now, whoever has been taught by the apostles has been taught to teach all that Jesus taught them, including the Modus Operandi.

HOMEWORK

1. For what purpose did Jesus come to planet earth? (I John 3:8)
2. What changed between the first thirty years and the last three years of His life? (Matthew 3:16, Acts 10:38, Luke 4:18, Isaiah 61:1-2, Isaiah 20:27)

ANOINTED: chriō (khree'-o)=through the idea of contact; to smear or rub with oil, that is, (by implication) to consecrate to an office or religious service: - anoint. G5530: chraomai=(khrah'-om-ahee)= to handle; to furnish what is needed; (give an oracle, graze [touch slightly], light upon, etc.), that is, (by implication) to employ or (by extension) to act towards one in a given manner: - entreat, use.

3. For what five things was Jesus anointed? (Luke 4:18-19, Isaiah 61:1-2)

•

•

•

•

•

•

4. After being baptized in water and The Holy Spirit (Matthew 3:13-17) Where was Jesus going throughout? Matthew 4:24)

5. When Jesus was going about in all of Galilee, was He doing good or bad? (Acts 10:38)

6. Who was going about like a lion seeking to devour and doing bad by harassing and oppressing people? (I Peter 5:8, Acts 10:38, AMP)

7. What were the three hallmarks of The Healer's Modus Operandi (M.O.)?

•

•

•

TEACHING: didaskō (did-as'-ko)=A prolonged (causative) form of a primary verb daō (to learn); to teach (in the same broadapplication): - teach.

TEACHING/PROCLAIMING: kērussō (kay-roos'-so)=Of uncertain affinity; to herald (as a public crier), especially divine truth (the gospel): - preach (-er), proclaim, publish.

HEALING: therapeuō (ther-ap-yoo'-o)= to wait upon menially, that is, (figuratively) to adore (God), or (specifically) to relieve (of disease): - cure, heal, worship.

8. Of what was Jesus healing? (Matthew 4:23)

HEALING: therapeuō (ther-ap-yoo'-o)=From the same as G2324; to wait upon menially, that is, (figuratively) to adore (God), or (specifically) to relieve (of disease): - cure, heal, worship. G2324: therapōn (ther-ap'-ohn)= a menial attendant (as if cherishing): - servant

9. How much of disease and sickness among the people was Jesus healing? (Matthew 4:23)

ALL MANNER: pas (pas)=Including all the forms of declension; apparently a primary word; all, any, every, the whole: - all (manner of, means) alway (-s), any (one), X daily, + ever, every (one, way), as many as, + no (-thing), X throughly, whatsoever, whole, whosoever.

10. Who was being brought to The Healer as news about Him spread about all Syria? (Matthew 4:22)

SICKNESS/ILL: nosos (nos'-os)==Of uncertain affinity; a malady (rarely figurative of moral disability): - disease, infirmity, sickness. (Matthew 4:24)

SICK: kakōs (kak-oce'=Adverb from G2556; badly (physically or morally): - amiss, diseased, evil, grievously, miserably, sick, sore. G2556: kakos (kak-os')=Apparently a primary word; worthless (intrinsically such; whereas G4190 properly refers to effects), that is, (subjectively) depraved, or (objectively) injurious: - bad, evil, harm, ill, noisome, wicked. (Matthew 4:25)

VARIOUS DIS-EASES:nosos=nos'-os=Of uncertain affinity; a malady (rarely figurative of moral disability): - disease, infirmity, sickness.

NOTE: Sickness is not limited to one dis-ase but various dis-eases. Each one is a curse that is overruled by the blessing.

"Also every sickness (various dis-eases) and every plague which is not written in the book of the law..."
Deuteronomy 28:61

PAINS/TORMENTS: basanos (bas'-an-os)= (through the notion of going to the bottom); a touch stone, that is, (by analogy) torture: - torment

DEMONIACS/POSSESSED WITH d-evils: daimonizomai (dahee-mon-id'-zom-ahee)=Middle voice from G1142; to be exercised by a daemon: - have a (be vexed with, be possessed with) devil (-s). G1142: daimōn (dah'ee-mown)=From daiō (to distribute fortunes); a demon or super natural spirit (of a bad nature): - devil.

EPILEPTICS/LUNATICS: seleniazomai

(sel-ay-nee-ad'-zom-ahee)Middle or passive voice from a presumed derivative of G4582= to be moon struck, that is, crazy: - be lunatic. G4582:selēnē (sel-ay'-nay)= through the idea of attractiveness); the moon: - moon.

PARALYTICS/PALSY: paralutikos (par-al-oo-tee-kos')=- From a derivative of G3886; as if dissolved, that is, paralytic: - that had (sick of) the palsy.G3886: paraluō (par-al-oo'-o)= to loosen beside, that is, relax (perfect passive participle paralyzed or enfeebled): - feeble, sick of the (taken with) palsy.

11. What did The Healer do to all who were brought to Him? (Matthew 4:24)

HEALED: therapeuō (ther-ap-yoo'-o)=From the same as G2324; to wait upon menially, that is, (figuratively) to adore (God), or (specifically) to relieve (of disease): - cure, heal, worship. G2324: therapōn (ther-ap'-ohn)=a menial attendant (as if cherishing) servant.

> *"How God anointed and consecrated Jesus (The Healer) of Nazareth with the (Holy) Spirit and with strength and ability and power (duNAmis, dynamic ability, power; how He went about (Modus Operandi, M.O.) and in particular curing all that were harassed and oppressed by [the power of] the d-evil, for God was with Him (The Healer)."*
>
> Acts 10:38, AMP
> with additions and emphasis mine

NOTE: The next set of questions are taken from The Amplified Bible. See above verse.

12. How many people did Jesus cure/heal? (Acts 10:38, AMP)
13. What was the sickness/dis-ease by the d-evil considered to be? (Acts 10:38, AMP)
14. What did The Healer do to the harassment and oppression of the d-evil? (Acts 10: 38, AMP)

CURING/HEALED: iaomai (ee-ah'-om-ahee)=Middle voice of apparently a primary verb; to cure (literally or figuratively): - heal, make whole.

15. Who was with The Healer as He healed? (Acts 10:38)
16. When the virgin was with child and bore a Son, what did they call His name? (Matthew 1:23, Isaiah 7:14)

IMMANUEL: Emmanouēl (em-man-oo-ale')=Of Hebrew origin [H6005]; God with us; Emmanuel, a name of Christ: - Emmanuel.

17. What is Immanuel translated to mean? (Matthew 4:23)
18. What other name did his earthly parents call Him?

JESUS: Iēsous (ee-ay-sooce')=Of Hebrew origin [H3091]; Jesus (that is, Jehoshua), the name of our Lord and two (three) other Israelites: - Jesus. H3091: yeh-ho-shoo'-ah, yeh-ho-shoo'-ah = Jehovah-saved; Jehoshua (that is, Joshua), the Jewish leader: - Jehoshua, Jehoshuah, Joshua.

NOTE: Jesus Immanuel was The Christ, The Anointed One, The Messiah who was anointed with yoke breaking, burden lifting, oppression removing, healing power of the anointing fo the Holy Ghost and Power.

The Modus Operandi (M.0.) was salvation demonstrated before the Death, Burial, Resurrection took place.

SALVATION: sōtēria (so-tay-ree'-ah)=Feminine of a derivative of G4990 as (properly abstract) noun; rescue or safety (physically or morally): - deliver, health, salvation, save, saving. G4990: sōtēr (so-tare')=From G4982; a deliverer, that is, God or Christ: savior. G4982: sōzō (sode'-zo)=to save, that is, deliver or protect (literally or figuratively): - heal, preserve, save (self), do well, be (make) whole.

NOTE: The Healer's Modus Operandi (M.0.) was to go about:
1. Rescuing
2. Physical and Moral safety
3. Deliverance/Deliver
4. Health/Heal
5. Salvation/Saving
6. Protection
7. Preservation
8. Make to do well
9. Making whole.

"Jesus Christ (The Anointed Healer) is the same yesterday, and today, and forever."
Hebrews 13:8

"The Healer healed yesterday, today and forever."
Hebrews 13:8

In our next chapter we will look at the woman who many

call, the woman with an issue of blood. I like to call her the healed woman because after an encounter with Jesus, she no longer had an issue of blood but was healed.

CHAPTER EIGHT

THE HEALED WOMAN

In Matthew 9:20-21, Mark 5:25-34, Luke 8:43-48 recounts the story of a woman who had an *issue of blood* for 12 years. I have always thought that she should be called The Healed Woman. She went from the point of a 12 year sickness to the point of *not being sick any longer* because as Jesus told her, "your faith has made you well." (Matthew 9:22)

> *"Jesus turned around and, seeing her, He said, 'take courage, daughter! Your faith has made your well. And at once the woman was restored to health."*
>
> Matthew 9:22, AMP
> with emphasis mine

There is a direct correlation between *faith and health.*

FAITH= The assurance, confirmation, title deed of things (healing) we hope for (have confident expectation) being the proof of things we *do not see* and the conviction of their reality, faith perceiving as real fact what is *not revealed to the senses.* (Hebrews 11:1, AMP)

The problem for this woman was that she had been *sick for*

12 years with an *issue (flow) of blood* that presented her with a social and religious stigma in her life. She was considered to unclean and not only was she isolated from the public, most likely she was unable to have children. This dis-ease also *wreaked havoc* (o cause damage, disruption, or destruction) with her financially as she saw multiple physicians she spent all she had. (Mark 5:26).

What changed in her life? She *heard* about Jesus. (Mark 5:27)

> *"So faith comes by hearing (what is told and what is heard comes by the preaching [of the message that came from the lips of Christ (the Messiah Himself)."*
>
> Romans 10:17
> with addition mine

As Jesus was doing His Modus Operandi thing, word spread throughout the country. I have to believe that this woman heard the word concerning Jesus and how He was healing all who were harassed and oppressed by the d-evil. I believe that something moved in here as doubt was replaced with hope (confident expectation) that she could possibly be healed of this issue of blood. I have to believe that she was sick and tired of being sick and tired. I have to believe that faith came to this woman and set into motion here next steps.

I always find it interesting that the woman began to speak to herself, over and over and over again.

> *"For she was saying to herself, if I only touch His garment I will get well."*
>
> Matthew 9:21

"For she kept saying to herself, if I only touch His garments I shall be restored to health."

Mark 5:28, AMP

SELF-TALK

Have you ever talked to yourself? I have, all the time. Sometimes I can talk my way into a rut of depression. I believe that is what she had done for 12 years until she heard words concerning Jesus, faith came, hope sprang alive and she began changing the way she was talking. She not only began to implement self-talk, she began to say it over and over again as she "kept saying to herself." (Matthew 9:20-22, Mark 5:27)

David, a man after God's own heart (I Samuel 13:14, Acts 13:22) knew the value of self-talk. I am thinking that we need to be renewing our minds more, begin speaking by faith for desired results and keep doing it until those desired results happens especially concerning healing.

"Yet we have the same spirit of faith as he had who wrote (David), I have believed, and therefore have I spoken. We to believe and therefore we speak."

II Corinthians 4:13, Psalm 116:10, AMP

"David was greatly distressed, for the men spoke of stoning him because the souls of them all were bitterly grieved, each man for his sons and daughters. But David encouraged and strengthened himself in the Lord His God."

I Samuel 30:6

David also sang about telling his soul what to do in Psalm

103:1-5. He told His soul to (1) Bless the Lord (2) Not to forget His benefits (including healing).

> "Bless the Lord O my soul, and all that is within me, bless His holy name. Bless the Lord, O my soul and forget none of His benefits..."
>
> Psalm 103:3-5

Those benefits included:
1. Who pardons all your iniquities
2. Who heals all your diseases
3. Who redeems your life from the pit
4. Who crowns you with lovingkindness and compassion
5. Who satisfies your years with good things so your youth is renewed like the eagle.

I believe that this is exactly what the woman with the issue of blood was doing to herself, even if she did not realize that she was doing it.

But she did not just talk about what she desired she took her faith and put into action. She got up off her sick bed and then proceeded to go find Jesus and do exactly what she kept on saying to herself, to reach out and touch His garments. Not only did she get off her sickbed and went outside, she pressed through the crowd who wanted healing and fought the press and the stigma of being (a) a woman (b) being unclean with and issue of blood.

Jesus was on the move as He went about all Galilee. As Jesus was going about He was:
1. Teaching in their synagogues from the book of Isaiah about the anointing that was one Him. (Isaiah 61:1-2, Luke 4:17-19, Acts 10:38)

2. Preaching the good news (Gospel) of the Kingdom, so faith could (and would) come.
3. Healing ALL who were ill, with various dis-eases, pains, demoniacs, epileptic, paralytics, and *He healed them.*

I am convinced that someone told this woman about Jesus and what He said and did, and faith came which that prompted her to action getting her off her sick bed and out of the house to put her faith in action. With *her faith* she:

1. She *kept saying to herself* if I only *touch* His garment (the hem or tassels), *I shall get well.*
2. She came up in the crowd behind Him through the crowd that was pressing around Him.
3. She did what she had been saying to herself over and over, she got down low (way down low) and reached out and touched the hem of His garment.

NOTE: Have you heard about Jesus the Healer? As faith has come to you (Romans 10:17 says it will come), how has that faith affected *your speech* (the way you talk) and how did that faith affect your *actions?*

The cause and effect of the woman's activated faith was that Jesus *saw* her faith and:

1. Jesus told her to *take courage* (be encouraged and not discouraged).
2. Jesus told her, Daughter (a covenant woman) *your faith* has made you well, go in peace, *be healed* of your affliction.
3. Immediately the hemorrhage stopped.

Because of Jesus, we all have a *healing covenant* with *Jehovah Raphe* (The Lord Who Heals). When you hear about Jesus and what He said about His Healing Anointing, begin to speak desired results (healing) to yourself (your soul) and forget none of His benefits including healing ALL your dis-eases (Psalm 103:1-3) and then take your faith and go from dead faith to alive faith by putting into motion corresponding actions.

HOMEWORK

(Matthew 9:20-21, Mark 5:25-34, Luke 8:43-48)

1. What disease did this woman have? (Matthew 9:20)
2. How long did she suffer with this problem. (Matthew 9:20)
3. What did she endure much at? (Mark 5:26)
4. How much money did she spend? (Mark 5:26)
5. How much was she helped? (Mark 5:26)
6. Did she get better or worse? (Mark 5:26)
7. Who could she not be healed by? (Luke 8:43)
8. When she touched the hem of His garment, what did Jesus say made her whole? (Matthew 9:22)

NOTE: When Jesus called her daughter, He was referring to the fact that she was a daughter under the Abrahamic Covenant, which had provision of healing for her, 12 years earlier.

9. From which direction did the woman approach Jesus in the crowd? (Mark 5:27)
10. What was the woman's thinking as she pressed through the crowd and touched His cloak? (Mark 5:27)
11. How quickly was the blood dried up once she touched His garment? (Mark 5:29)
12. What did she physically feel in her body when she touched His garment? (Mark 5:29)
13. What was this sickness, this issue of blood, this hemorrhage considered to be? (Mark 5:29)

14. When she touched His garment, what did Jesus perceive/feel? (Mark 5:30)

15. What did Jesus ask as the power proceeded out of Him? (Mark 5:30)

16. What was the disciple's response to the question by Jesus? (Mark 5:30)

17. Once the woman was aware of what had happened to her, and she told Jesus it was her and she told Him the whole truth, what did Jesus say had made her well? (Mark 5:33-34)

18. What were Jesus' instructions to her? (Mark 5:34)

19. Again, what did Jesus consider this thing that she was healed of to be? (Mark 5:34)

20. What part of Jesus' cloak did she reach out and touch? (Luke 8:44)

NOTE: According the note on Luke 8:44 in the Ryrie Study Bible Commentary:

The Fringe of His cloak: A tassel that a rabbi wore on his outer garment. The garment was draped over the back so that the tassel of one corner hung between the shoulder blades."

21. What did the disciples tell Jesus that the people were doing? (Luke 8:45)

22. Jesus told the disciples that someone had touched Him. What was Jesus aware of when the woman had touched Him? (Luke 8:45)

NOTE: I submit to you that yes, everyone was touching Jesus but the woman's touch was a touch of faith that she received when she heard about Jesus healing, when she kept on saying that if she would touch His garment she would be made well, that as she got off of her sickbed, went outside, fought the crowd, got way down low to reach through and touch the hem of His garment, she was healed.

23. One last time, what did Jesus say had made her well/ whole, His healing virtue or her faith? (Luke 8:48)

WELL/WHOLE: sōzō (sode'-zo) = safe; to *save*, that is, *deliver* or *protect* (literally or figuratively): - heal, preserve, save (self), do well, be (make) whole.

24. What did Jesus tell her to go in? (Luke 8:48)

PEACE: eirēnē (i-rah'-nay) = (to *join*); *peace* (literally or figuratively); by implication *prosperity:* - one, peace, quietness, rest, + set at one again.

NOTE: This woman who for 12 years at been under the thumb of poverty, disjointed, unrest, was now set at one again, like she was 12 years earlier before the issue of blood began. He was healed as Jesus demonstrated the will of God on earth as it was in heaven. If you look up to heaven there is no issue of blood (hemorrhage) in heaven.

Now you know why I call this woman "the healed woman" instead of the "woman with the issue of blood.

In our next chapter we will look at healing as a blessing and not a curse.

CHAPTER NINE

THE BLESSING OF HEALING

I n the Old Testament we see that not only are there "*ten Commandments*" (also known as the *ten words* or the *Decalogue (Dekalog)* but there are 613 plus laws, rules and regulations that if you don't keep them you are cursed. I find it interesting that while there are "ten commandments" (Exodus 31:18, Exodus 25:25:21, Deuteronomy 10:2, 5) the following chapters in Exodus expounds upon those commandments. It is like a company with a Policy and Procedure handbook where, the policy "the Ten Commandments" are listed and then the policy is explained and clarified with the procedure.

> "*The Talmud notes that the Hebrew numerical value (gematria) of the word "Torah" is 611, and combining Moses's 611 commandments with the first two of the Ten Commandments which were the only ones heard directly from God, adds up to 613.*"
>
> Wikipedia

Healing is a blessing. Healing is life. Healing is the will of God.

BLESSING: berâkâh (ber-aw-kaw') =From H1288;

benediction; by implication *prosperity:* - blessing, liberal, pool, present. H1288: bârak (*baw-rak'*) =A primitive root; to *kneel*; by implication to *bless* God (as an act of adoration), and (vice-versa) man (as a benefit); also (by euphemism) to *curse* (God or the king, as treason): - X abundantly, X altogether, X at all, blaspheme, bless, congratulate, curse, X greatly, X indeed, kneel (down), praise, salute, X still, thank.

Sickness is a curse. Sickness is death. Sickness is the will of the d-evil.

CURSE; qelâlâh (kel-aw-law') =From H7043; *vilification:* - (ac-) curse (-d, -ing). H7043: qâlal (kaw-lal) =A primitive root; to *be* (causatively *make*) *light*, literally (*swift, small, sharp,* etc.) or figuratively (*easy, trifling, vile,* etc.): - abate, make bright, bring into contempt, (ac-) curse, despise, (be) ease (-y, -ier), (be a, make, make somewhat, move, seem a, set) light (-en, -er, ly, -ly afflict, -ly esteem, thing), X slight [-ly], be swift (-er), (be, be more, make, re-) vile, whet.

> *"How God (not the d-evil) anointed (poured out, rubbed in, smeared upon) and consecrated (set aside for a purpose) Jesus (salvation) of Nazareth with the (Holy) Spirit and power (duNAmis, dynamic ability): how He (Jesus the Healer, God in the flesh) went about doing good (and not bad) and in particular (more specifically) curing ALL (everyone who was healed) that were harassed and oppressed (not blessed but cursed) by [the power] of the d-evil (NOT by God) for God was with Him (Immanuel=God With Us)."*
>
> Acts 10:38, AMP
> with emphasis and addition mine

If Acts 10:38 is true *and it is*, then why would we ever accept a *curse* of sickness and try and convince ourselves that it is a blessing? What a wonderful choice they had in the Old Testament (the Fat Part of the Book) and what an even better choice we have in the New Testament (The Skinny Part of the Book) as we choose life/blessing over death/curse!!!! Jesus hung on a tree, the cross and became a curse so we would have a choice of curse or blessing, sin or salvation, sickness or healing.

> *"I call Heaven and earth to witness this day against you that I have set before you, life and death, the blessing and the curse; therefore choose life (why?) that you and our descendants my live; to love the Lord your God, to obey His voice, and to cling to Him; for He is your life, and the length of your days that you may dwell in the land (of Promise) which the Lord swore to give (Covenant Promise) your fathers, to Abraham, Isaac, and Jacob (and to you and me through Jesus)."*

Deuteronomy 30:19-20, AMP
with emphasis and addition mine

> *"So then, those who are His people are blessed and made happy and favored by God [as partners in fellowship] with the believing and trusting Abraham (covenant man). And all who depend on the Law (versus grace, free gift, free favor, the divine influence manifested in the life)--who are seeking to be justified by obedience to the Law of rituals--are under a curse (not a blessing) and doomed (cause and effect of the curse) to disappointment and destruction; for it is written in the Scriptures (Deuteronomy 27:26) "cursed (accursed,*

devoted to destruction, doomed to eternal punishment) be everyone who does not continued to abide (live and remain) by all the precepts and commands written in the book of the Law, and practice them."

Galatians 3:9-10

In my study of the Pentateuch (1st Five Books of the Fat Part of the Book), the books of Moses, there are at least 613 Laws to follow. Jesus did not come to destroy the Law but to fulfill the Law. (Matthew 5:17-20) Thank God, because I could not handle 10 commandments much less 613. In my studies of the Old Testament, I would constantly write in big letters *Jesus* or D.B.R. (Death Burial, Resurrection) on the tree. As I studied through Deuteronomy 28 (where the curses and blessings are listed) I would write I AM BLESSED, I CHOOSE BLESSING, (again written in big, bold letters in my Bible)

HOMEWORK

1. What was promised to come on the children of Israel? (Deuteronomy 28:2)
2. What was required for these blessings to come on them? (Deuteronomy 28:2)
3. These blessing were promise not only to come on them but also promised to what? (Deuteronomy 28:2)
4. Where would they be blessed? (Deuteronomy 28:3)
5. What would be blessed? (Deuteronomy 28:4)
6. What two things would be blessed? (Deuteronomy 28:4)
7. What will the Lord cause with this blessing?

(Deuteronomy 28:6)

8. How will this blessing manifest itself in the face of the enemies? (Deuteronomy 28:7)

9. What will the Lord command His blessing upon? (Deuteronomy 28:8)

10. What will the Lord establish? (Deuteronomy 28:9)

11. With this blessing what will all the earth see? (Deuteronomy 28:10)

12. What will the Lord make abound with this blessing? (Deuteronomy 28:11)

13. What will the Lord open for the blessed? (Deuteronomy 28:12)

14. What will be the cause and effect of blessing on the land and work? (Deuteronomy 28:12)

15. What will you do to many nations and not do? (Deuteronomy 28:12)

16. What will the blessed be/ not be? (Deuteronomy 28:13)

17. What is the condition for these blessings to be active in their lives. (Deuteronomy 28:13-14)

NOTE: Deuteronomy 28:15-26 lists the cause and effect of the curse and not obeying the Lord.

SICKNESS IS A CURSE AND NOT A BLESSING

In Deuteronomy 28:220-61 we see various sicknesses and diseases listed as a curse. We do not see these listed in Deuteronomy 28:1-14 under the blessings, because sicknesses and diseases are not a blessing, but they are a curse.

1. Confusion
2. Pestilence

3. Consumption
4. Fever
5. Inflammation
6. Blight with mildew
7. Boils of Egypt
8. Tumors (emrods aka hemorrhoids)
9. The scab
10. Itch (cannot be healed)
11. Madness
12. Blindness
13. Bewilderment of heart
14. Blindness
15. Driven mad by the sight of what you see
16. Sore boils on your knees and legs
17. Sore boils from your foot to the crown of your head
18. Extraordinary plagues
19. Miserable and chronic sickness
20. All the disease of Egypt
21. Every sickness and every plague which, not written in the book of the law.

NOTE: The phrase in Deuteronomy 28:61 says, "...the Lord will bring on you until you are destroyed. Many theologians believes this read, "...the Lord will PERMIT to come on you...." For me this is consistent with the nature of God blessing and not cursing. The curse occurs when you walk away from the blessing and don't do what He says. When you don't do as He says (aka obedience) it opens the door to the cures.

NOTE: Well, it is apparent to me that out of the 600+ things that we have to obey (not counting all the other rules and regulations put on us by man) that we cannot keep the law. Something had to take place to bring us to the place of blessing. That something was actually a someone named Jesus.

HOW TO BE REDEEMED FROM THE CURSE AND ENTER INTO THE BLESSING

"Christ redeemed you from the curse of the Law, having become a curse for us—for it is written, cursed is everyone who hangs on a tree (Deuteronomy 21:3) , in order (the purpose for the tree and someone to hang on that tree) in Christ Jesus, the blessing of Abraham (not the curse of the law) might come to the Gentiles (non-covenant people), so that we would receive the promise of the Spirit through faith."

Galatians 3:13-14
with addition mine

Obedience to the law is fulfilled in everything that Jesus did on the cross. We now access the blessings by faith in His Word. Every area of the curse has been dealt with on the Cross and by faith I enter into the blessings, not only of Abraham but God.

In the next chapter I will tell you the story of what happened to me on June 14th 2017 when I had a cerebellum stroke. I have taught for years on the will of God concerning healing and suddenly I was face with sickness and death. The next chapter is called, What Do You Do When You Teach and Believe in Healing and Then You Get Sick.

CHAPTER TEN

WHAT DO YOU DO WHEN YOU BELIEVE AND TEACH HEALING
AND THEN YOU BECOME SICK?

"You know you are an author when you have a stroke and you consider your trip to the hospital as research for you book on healing."

Rodney Lewis Boyd, author

PHASE ONE (In The Beginning)

I was in the process of writing this book about healing, and then I was surprised by having a stroke which I would learn later was a cerebellar stroke, and now I am a chapter in my own book. What the d-evil meant for harm has backfired on him. The one who oppresses people with sickness and disease tried to put out the fire of proclamation and declaration that God is the healer, but taking what he thought was a bucket of water and throwing it over me but it turned out to be a bucket of gasoline and KABOOM, the passion of proclaiming Jesus as healer flamed up. Here is my story, as best as I can remember it, with help from my wife Brenda filling in the details.

On *June 15th 2017* it was a morning like any other morning. I woke up at 5:00 in the morning, drank some coffee, checked Facebook, read the Bible, prayed, and kissed Brenda good-bye. It was just another Thursday.

I ate breakfast which included microwaved frozen meatballs, with hot sauce, barbeque sauce with cheddar cheese on top microwaved to perfection. Ah, the breakfast of champions. I got in the shower to get ready for work with anticipation of a full day of patients to see and *suddenly* the shower walls started to spin like a carnival ride. I appeared to be having an episode of vertigo. In an effort to stop the spinning I put my hand on one wall and my other hand on the other wall. The spinning did not stop but seemed to intensify. Without warning the entire shower appeared to turn on its side and it seemed to me that I was thrown to the shower floor hitting my back on the spigot and just lying there in a daze. In reality I fell down in the shower floor.

I finally reached up to turn off the water which was beginning to turn cold. I must have been laying there for a while. I tried to reason how to get out of the tub but all I could think of was how impossible it seemed. I eventually swung my leg over the side of the tub and with great effort pulled myself out of the shower. Once I overcame the barrier of the side of the tub I flopped down into the bathroom floor. Somehow I stood up and eased my way to the bedroom. At this point my memory is getting hazy but I do I remember grabbing a garbage pail and started throwing up. Somehow I made my way back to the bedroom and I remember that I flopped back on the bed thinking that I was a mass of sweat, however in retrospect it could be that I was still wet from the shower water coming down on me. From this point and for the next twelve days Brenda filled me in on the gaps in my memory.

When Brenda came home she said that I was fully clothed which I have no recollection about putting on my clothes. I did not call anyone and don't remember anything until Brenda came home from work earlier than normal at around 1:00 P.M. I barely remember her quizzing me about what was going on and it seems like we determined that it was just vertigo, like Phillip our son had when he was in high school. We were going to the doctor the next morning to check it out. At this time Brenda has told me that I was awake, alert and conversing with her. Time passed and again I don't remember a lot of what took place. Apparently a few hours passed and it was time to go to bed. Again, I don't remember anything even though I appeared to be cognizant and conversing with Brenda. Time passed and it was time to go to bed for the night.

Brenda told me not to get up in the middle of the night to use the bathroom unless I woke her up. Of course, I had to utilize the facilities and reasoned that I was feeling better so I got up without waking Brenda made my way to the bathroom, did my business and made my way back to bed. Ah sweet success. Later on that night the same thing occurred, except this time I was stumbling towards the bathroom and fell face first into the bathtub busting my mouth and nose with blood everywhere. Brenda appeared instantly and comforted me with the words, "I thought I told you to wake me." I believe I actually remembered this but things are still fuzzy.

I finally got back to bed after Brenda cleaned me up of the blood from my mouth and nose, however we were still thinking that it was vertigo and that we would go to the doctor in the morning and get a shot and some medication. At this point it never occurred to us that I had experienced a stroke.

The next morning Brenda had to go to work for a hospital case until she could get somebody to replace her. She was not gone very long. Again, it appeared that I was doing better and was still cognizant and conversing with her. She called Phillip to come over and help her get me into the car to go to the doctor. When Phillip had his episode of vertigo years ago when he was in high school he reminded his mom that it took both of us over an hour or more just to get him downstairs because of the vertigo. Phillip had the wisdom to tell his mom "no" and to call for an ambulance, which she did.

The ambulance came along with a firetruck in our driveway. One of the last things I remembered for the next twelve days was the EMTs coming into the bedroom with a stretcher and they transferred me from the bed to the stretcher. They took me to Saint Thomas Medical Center in Murfreesboro where I was in a room within the Emergency Room for a couple of hours. During this time they took me for a CT scan to check out my injuries to my nose and mouth when I fell and hit my face on the side of the bathtub. It was during this time that they saw that I had a cerebellar stroke which was at the base of the brainstem. Now, as a Speech-Language Pathologist, I have worked with hundreds of people who have experienced a stroke. The most common strokes occur either on the side of the brain. On the left side of the brain is where the speech-language and hearing centers are located. On the right side of the brain is where cognition and reasoning can be affected. On each side of the brain, in the right and left hemisphere there are motor strips that affects speech with dysarthria or slurred speech. The nature of the event is that if the stroke takes place on the left side of the brain, the opposite of the face or body can be weakened or paralyzed and the reverse if it occurs on the right side of the brain, the left side is affected. The stroke had occurred in the cerebellum on the left side due to a possible blockage. The cerebellum is located at the base of the brain stim and is known as "the drunk stroke" because it affects balance and mimics being drunk. Balance and equilibrium were affected which included the vertigo at the initial time of the stroke.

Brenda called the surgery center to report that a stroke had occurred. One of her co-workers at the surgery center, a nurse anesthesiologist told her to get me to Saint Thomas Nashville immediately. A doctor came by to check on me and Brenda voiced her desire for me to be moved. The neurologist also came by and concurred that it would be best for me to be moved. They reasoned that if I needed surgery like the removal of the plate from the back of my head to ease the pressure of the swelling of the brain, that they would be unable to do that surgery in Murfreesboro. During this time Bruce and Jill Coble came to offer their support to me and Brenda. As the word got out, the prayer wheels were set into motion.

They placed me in an ambulance and off we went to Saint Thomas West. Brenda, my son Phillip and his wife Jamie followed the ambulance and by the time they arrived, they already had me in a room with I.V. going. Wow what a difference from laying in the emergency room for two hours in Murfreesboro to being in ICU in Nashville immediately.

I was in the Intensive Care Unit for nine days and then transferred to a regular room for three days before my discharge to in-patient rehabilitation.

Again, at this point I don't remember very much and Brenda and friends have been helping me peel back the onion and filling in the gaps in my memory. Left to my own devices when I try to tell the story I tend to embellish the facts. Over the next few days friends and family came to see me of whom I remember very little about their visit.

PHASE TWO (The Intensive Care Unit)

For the next nine days I was in the intensive care unit and then was transferred to a regular room. Of the twelve day I remember very little. Sometimes when I am telling the story of these days, Brenda will stop me and say, "*It didn't happen that way.*" So, know that the facts have been checked before they were placed in this chapter. Thank God for Brenda and anyone who came to visit me while I was in the hospital and specifically in the intensive care unit.

Prior to the stroke (not mine, I do not claim it or take ownership of the harassment and oppression by the d-evil) although, I do accept my stupidity for poor diet, minimal exercise, etc.), I had taught and requested from those taught (concerning healing) that if I ever got sick and went into the hospital, do not come to the hospital and visit me with doubt and unbelief. Do not pray that the "will of God" unless you believe that the "will of God on earth as it is in heaven" was healing. Since the stroke I have looked very hard up to heaven and as of this writing I have not found strokes, diabetes, heart difficulties, cancer, arthritis (fill in the blank of any sickness) in heaven.

As the word leaked out, many prayers bombarded heaven from many places around the world. My pastor, Allen Jackson (no not the singer) was leading a group/tour in Israel and they prayed. It has been said that if you pray from America, it is a "long distance call" but in Israel it is a "local call." Men, women, children were praying prayers of faith. Obviously, I was not praying for myself, or at least I don't remember doing it. Maybe my spirit (little s) within me was interceding via the Holy Spirit.

SHAMELESS SELF PROMOTION AND COMMER-CIAL BREAK

If you are interested in my other books including:
1. *Never Run A Dead Kata (Lessons I Learned In The Dojo)*
2. *Pro-Verb Ponderings (31 Ruminations on Positive Action)*
3. *Speaking and Hearing The Word of God (A Speech-Language Pathologist Perspective)*
4. *Chewing the Daily Cud (Volume 1)*
5. *Chewing the Daily Cud (Volume 2)*
6. *Chewing the Daily Cud (Volume 3)*
7. *Chewing the Daily Cud (Volume 4)*
8. *Written That You May Believe (21 Things To Believe From The Gospel of John)*

These books are available for purchase from Amazon, Barnes and Noble, WordCrafts Press. They are also available in various forms of e-books including Kindle and Nook.

You may also access my books by my website at www.rodneylewisboyd.com

There are also lots of goodies that you can explore on the site. I would like to give a shout out to Bryan Entzminger who captured my vision for the website and brought it to life.

WE NOW RETURN TO YOUR READING OF *ON EARTH AS IT IS IN HEAVEN (Healing 101)*

While lying in bed at the hospital in the intensive care unit I had many visitors flowing in and out including, family, friends, doctors, nurses, therapist and various hospital staff. According to Brenda, most of them were wonderful.

A FEW STORIES TO TELL

I will limit many of the stories to just a few. Each one speaks to me about the "goodness of God in the land of the living."

Psalm 27:13

Initial Arrival

I was transferred from the hospital in Murfreesboro Tennessee to one in Nashville Tennessee. A lady that Brenda worked with at a surgery center told her to get me out of the one in Murfreesboro and down to Nashville. The physician's in Murfreesboro agreed. By the time Brenda, Phillip and Jamie got down to the hospital in Nashville I was already in a room in ICU and hooked up to I.V's being seen by the Stroke Team. I had been in the E.R. area for a couple of hours previously due to no room in the facility. I did have a CT Scan where they found the cerebellum stroke.

My Physical Condition

During the nine days in ICU, for the most part, I was awake, alert, cooperative, cognitive and talking making sense. On the surface you could not tell I had a stroke, although you could tell something was not right. On day three, I took a turn for the worse and was not responding at all. This is when Brenda was told that if the swelling of the brain (the cerebellum and surrounding area) did not go down, the prognosis was that (1) I would die (2) They needed to consider Hospice. The physicians told Brenda, Phillip and Jamie that they needed to have a family meeting to discuss my options. The prognosis was not good, but faith does not come by prognosis but by hearing and hearing the Word of God concerning Christ. (Romans 10:17)

NOTE: Somewhere in my mind I have thought that they were told, if I didn't die I would be paralyzed from the neck down. Brenda says she does not remember this, but it does make for a good story. Take it with a grain of salt as something in the mind of someone who had a stroke.

Cause and Effect

Many have asked what caused the stroke. There most likely are many variables that contributed to the stroke. A big part of the problem can be traced back to poor dietary habits. As a home health Speech Pathologist, I drive a lot. At the time I was driving from Cannon County to Coffee County, to Bedford County to Franklin County to Moore County. There were lots of driving and lots of stops at fast food places and convenience stores for snacks. My diet was an overload of carbohydrates from burgers, chips, candy and to neutralize it was diet soft drinks. While I was in the process of losing weight and did some exercise, it all took a toll on my body. When the stroke occurred, they found that my blood sugar was up in the 400's to 500's with an A1C of 15.3 with 7.0 being normal. The physician said they do not know if it was the stroke that caused the elevated blood sugar or the blood sugar caused the stroke." The bottom line is it happened.

GODISNOWHERE

Brenda tells me that I had wrote (or had someone write) down GODISNOWHERE on a piece of paper and later had it written down on the white board in the room. I would then ask everyone who came in to read it for me. They would normally read God is NO where to which I would reply read it again to which they would read God is NOW here. I would respond that it all depends on how you look at it with the eyes of doubt or the eyes of faith. I was a witness not knowing I was a witness. In Acts 1:8 it says, "You shall receive power (dynamic ability) after the Holy Ghost has come upon you and you shall BE my witnesses…."To "be" a witness is a noun and it is who you are. To witness is a verb and it is what you do. In the words of Mike Gibson, who is now with Jesus, "This is who we are, this is what we do." Apparently, I was doing it not knowing I was doing it.

The Sternum Rub

During this time when I was not responding, there was a nurse that sat on the side of the bed and began to do a sternal rub. "A sternum rub is the application of painful stimuli with the knuckles of closed fist to the center chest of a patient who is not alert and does not respond to verbal stimuli." (www.ems1.com) In my mind as I tell this story, I say that the nurse hopped on top of me in the bed and straddled my chest and began the sternum rub. Of course it did not happen that way as Brenda is quick to correct me. As stated, at the beginning of this section, she sat on the side of the bed, but my story is more exciting. The only thing that aroused me is when my friend Trent Messick would say loudly, "Rodney!" I would arouse momentarily.

The Lifelines

During this down time, Brenda, as strong as she was and is, was being overwhelmed. Trent and Laura Messick, dear friends and brother and sister in the Lord became Brenda's lifeline. They were there to pray and support Brenda at this time. Laura had a word of wisdom to get music going in the room because that was the language that I understand. So they got my phone and began playing everything I had on my phone including Elvis Presley, various Christian artists and styles, and Kenneth Hagin reading Healing Scriptures. In retrospect this was a turn-around moment in my recovery.

Many people came to visit me but I don't remember any of them in that 12 day period. People like pastor of Springhouse Worship and Arts center came, prayed and sang to me. Bruce and Jill Coble came when I first went into the hospital for prayer support. Wayne Berry who at the time was worship pastor at Springhouse came and sang Elvis and other songs in my ears and prayed. I keep finding out about others who came that I just don't remember but they were encouragement for Brenda and the family.

King of the Whole Wide World

One song that I vaguely remember was Elvis Presley's

song from the movie *Kid Galahad, King Of The Whole Wide World*. I remember thinking that this was a song of faith. It speaks of a poor man who wants an oyster while the rich man wants the pearl in the oyster but in the contrast is the man who can sing when he does not have a thing he is to be known as a king of the whole wide world. At that point I did not have a thing health wide but by faith I was a king who served the King of Kings.

The Return

Apparently from what Brenda tells me, I was out for a couple of day but at some point, I woke up and slowly returned was awake again and slowly returned back to where I was before the downturn a few days earlier.

While I was out of it, Brenda was praying and the Lord spoke to her and said to her, "I have heard your prayers and answered." It was moments like these that became points of encouragement as she walked by faith and not by sight. By sight there appeared to be no hope, no confident expectation, but by faith the was hope.

As a Speech-Language Pathologist, part of my job was to do cognitive evaluations and the doctor came in and did what I do to many people. He asked me to repeat three word, a truck, a train, and huckleberry. According to Brenda I repeated the first two words and then attempted to lift my head towards the doctor and said, "I'll be your huckleberry". For those not familiar this is what Doc Holiday said in the movie Tombstone. The doctor looked at Brenda and said, "What did he say?" Brenda responded, "I think he said he will be your huckleberry". It was at this point that Brenda knew that I was back.

I'm Thirsty

At this time, in the earlier days of this stroke, they were trying to reduce the swelling of the brain with a drug called Mannitol. This is a saline/sugar based solution. After a few days I was very thirsty and I told the doctor that I needed something to drink. He told me that I would have to have a Speech Therapist to clear me to eat and drink. Brenda said I got adamant and said, "I AM a Speech Therapist and I say I can drink!" His response was that I could have a (singular) ice chip every 15 minutes.

At one point Brenda had to leave for some reason and while she was gone, I spied some snacks somewhere in the room and I had my friend Gary Montgomery (along with his wife Rena) to bring the bag over because I was hungry. Gary didn't realize the restrictions so he brought me the bag and I began to scarf them down. Brenda came in and corrected that situation very quickly.

Arrival of The Speech-Language Pathologist

One of the many jobs that a Speech-Language Pathologist does is to clear the patient to be given food and/or drink. Brenda tells me that I had around a 45 minute conversation with her about the mechanics of swallowing, speech therapy, various teachers in schools, etc. Of course, once again I don't remember her or the conversations. She eventually cleared me to eat and drink.

A few months later I was at a Speech conference and in the class we were talking about how people are in the hospital and sometimes the swallowing evaluation is delayed due to a Speech Pathologist is not available over the weekend and how this would delay the patient from having food or drink for a few days because no one was there who could clear them to eat or drink. I relayed my story to them (adding in some humor). At the break for that session a lady came up to me and told me that she could say that my story was true, because she was my Speech Pathologist who had the conversation. That is one of those God moments.

Rehab and Beyond

When released from the hospital I went to (1) Vanderbilt Stallworth Rehabilitation Hospital for a couple of weeks and then to (2) Pi Beta Phi outpatient rehab at Vanderbilt. Each one has many stories to tell but that may be for another time. I will say that at St. Thomas Hospital (West), Stallworth Hospital, and Pi Beta Phil Outpatient Rehabilitation, they had wonderful Physical Therapists, Occupational Therapists and Speech-Language Pathologists. I never had to have Speech during the whole time. Thanx and a Tip O Da Hat to Robert McPeters and Bruce Coble for driving me to outpatient rehab.

Suffice to say, I progressively got better and was discharged to home. I was released from Vanderbilt Stallworth Rehabilitation Hospital on July 14th 2017, which was our 45 wedding anniversary.

What a blessing it was. I was still not 100 % but a lot better. They gave me things to do on my own. As of this writing I am 95% better, still get light headed and dizzy at times but better. I was eventually released to drive.

The Blood Sugar Connection

As stated before the blood sugar was out of whack and the physicians are not sure if it was the high blood sugar that caused the stroke or if the stroke caused the high blood sugar. Whatever it was, I had high blood sugar after the stroke. I am unsure of the initial numbers but it was 400+ for the blood sugar readings with the A1C readings being at 15.3, with 7.0 being normal. At some point during my stay I was on four shots of insulin on a sliding scale which was given for the convenience of the nurses. When I returned home I went to an endocrinologist that had a nutritionist in the practice.

Since the visit to the endocrinologist and the nutritionist my blood sugars have been progressively getting better to the point of three of the insulin shots being discontinued. I am currently taking one shot of insulin in the morning and metformin 2 times a day. I have also changed my dietary habits watching carbs and attempting to increase exercise (which is a struggle). The A1C has progressively declined: 15.3, 14.5, 6.9, 6.6, 6.1.

As I attack the diabetes problems on the physical level I am aggressively fighting it on a spiritual level. On the spiritual level,

1. I am renewing my mind with the Word of God concerning supernatural healing.
2. I am practicing Romans 4:17-21, where Abraham had a promise of a child that was delayed coming. Abraham
   - In hope against hope, believed
   - Without becoming weak in faith he contemplated his own body, now as good as dead since it was about a

hundred year old, and the deadness of Sarah's womb (Romans 4:19) When it says "he contemplated his own body", it means he took stock of the reality of his old worn out physical being.

- YET, with respect to the promise of God he DID NOT WAVER IN UNBELIEF
- Instead of wavering in UNBELIEF He GREW STRONG IN FAITH giving glory to God
- He gave glory to God
- He was FULLY ASSSURED/PERSUADED that what God had promised, He was able to perform.
- He knew the God who gives life to the dead and CALLS INTO BEING THAT WHICH DOES NOT EXIST. Many versions say it this way, "He calls things that are NOT as though they were.

Where many are concerning healing they call things that ARE as if they will never change. With this in mind, I have begun to speak to my body as a mountain and tell it specifically what to do. Every time I take my medication I speak out loud, "I thank God that I am NOT a diabetic. I thank You Lord that my blood sugars are normal, I thank you Lord that my A1C readings are within normal limits. I thank you Lord that my pancreas and liver functions like it was designed to function. I never personalize the dis-ease. I never say my diabetes, my stroke, my (fill in the blank).

Ever since I have been doing this I am seeing a progressive decline in my numbers. The A1C readings have gone from 4.5 down to 6.1 where 7.0 is normal. Blood Sugars keep coming down on a more consistent level. I do the same thing with the lingering effects of the stroke like feeling imbalanced.

Weight Loss

When Brenda and I first started dating back in 1969 I weighed a whopping 136 pounds. Over the years I ballooned up to 325+ pounds. I lost down to 287 pounds and stayed there for years. Around 2 years ago, I joined Weight Watchers (again) with a goal to lose down to 200 pounds. Into the process I lost down to 230 pounds and then the stroke occurred. Since the stroke I lost down to 188 pounds and now am leveling off between 190 and 205. While the stroke was horrible, the weight loss is a good thing.

Retirement

During this time on September 1st, I officially retired. At some point Brenda encouraged me to go back to work at my old job two days a week because I was spending too much time watching the T.V. show, Gunsmoke. Can you really watch too much Gunsmoke? I now work two days a week (seeing a limited amount of patients) and I am off on Mondays, Tuesdays, and Wednesdays. I have time to write, play music, met people eat lunch. I also do housework, cook and get ready for Brenda to come home. Brenda says when I met people for lunch it is called ROMEO, Retired Old Men Eating Out.

Final Thoughts...Finally

Well, that's my story and I am sticking to it. There are so many stories and people who came to see me and have prayed for me that I don't remember but I am forever grateful to them all. I am especially grateful to Brenda who stayed by my side from the beginning until now. I am also so grateful to be around to see the birth or our first granddaughter Emerson Grace Boyd born to my son Phillip and his wife Jamie. I am overwhelmed with the feeling that this life is so precious and that life is too short to waste time on things that just don't matter.

I hope this chapter and actually the whole book will be a source of encouragement to press into the God of possibility as you are faced with impossibilities of life, whatever they may be.

HOMEWORK

While this chapter was more narrative about my own personal experience, there are a few Scriptures that spoke to me before, during and after this entire process.

Chapter Eleven

DIABETES (Reality Versus Truth)

DISCLAIMER: I know that many STRONG believers in the Lord, believe that whatever happens, happens for a purpose and sickness is from God, but I don't believe it. I believe The Will of God is Healing (going from the point of being sick to the point of being sick no longer) and that sickness is nothing but harassment and oppression by the d-evil. (Acts 10:38). Can you get to heaven without believing in healing? Yes, you just may get there quicker.

"There are about 100,000 human diseases that have been identified in this World. Out of the known 100,000 diseases, diabetes, a group of diseases that result in too much sugar in the blood (high blood glucose) is one of them.

People handled this CURSE in many different ways. Many accept it as the will of God or some punishment for their lifestyle, some ignore it and allow it to get worse and manifest itself with everything from strokes to amputation of body parts. Some regulate it by medication, diet and exercises. At times this hellish disease can be reversed while at other times it becomes a life time curse. Some accept the d-evil's harassment and oppression as the will of God (not true). Just because something happens does not mean that it is the will of God. I do know that diabetes is covered under

Deuteronomy 28:61 a a curse. No doubt the Lord will allow a cursed but it is not His perfect will.

> *"How God anointed and consecrated Jesus of Nazareth (The Healer) with the Holy Spirit and with strength and ability (dynamic) and power (duNAmis); how He (The Healer) went about (Matthew 4:23-24) doing good (not bad) and in particular , curing (healing) ALL who were harassed and oppressed (by sickness, dis-ease, dis-comfort, dys-function) by [the power of] the d-evil, for God was with Him (The Healer), (Immanuel, God with us)."*

Acts 10:38, AMP
with emphasis and addition mine

I believe that we have exousia (delegated authority) and and duNAmis (dynamic ability) to access by FAITH God's will on earth (where there is diabetes) AS IT IS (just like it is) in heaven (where there is no diabetes).

I suggest that IF you are plagued with diabetes that you take an active and aggressive stance in the Spirit by faith against the d-evil's diabetes. Yes, eat right, yes take the medicine BUT YES begin to speak to the mountain of d-evil diabetes and and tell the d-vil diabetes where to go. Call things that are NOT (the diabetes) as though they were (healed).

When I had the stroke (will never call it mine because the d-evil is the author of sickness and dis-ease) my blood sugar shot up to 485+ with an A1C of 14.5. I was placed on 4 shots of insulin on a sliding scale. I had listened to a teaching by Kate McVeigh called "calling things which be not as though they were." I began to implement the principles in the teaching for my physical being. I began to speak to my body every time I took the medicine. (currently off of three shots of insulin) I would (and still do) say, "I thank God that I am not a diabetic. I thank God that my blood sugar levels and A1C levels are normal. I thank God that my pancreas and liver functions."

The A1C (reflective of 3 month average of blood sugar levels) has gone progressively down from:

1. 15.8
2. 14.5
3. 6.9
4. 6.6
5. 6.1

Normal is 7.0, but of course the doctor's want it lower and so do I. I keep speaking, keep believing and keep hoping with confident expectation. If this is denial it is because I deny the d-evil and reality the right to rule me.

The struggle is real. As of this writing, I am still walking by FAITH and not by SIGHT as I expect total healing of diabetes. I still state by faith as I inject myself that, "I am not a diabetic." I still speak to the mountains of A1C to go below 6.0. I still speak to the mountain of blood sugar readings to normalize in the name of Jesus. However, I still see symptoms and signs of diabetes when I check my blood sugar on my monitor. I do not walk by SIGHT but I do walk by FAITH. At the same time, I really do believe that the Lord has given our bodies the ability to heal itself, especially when we do the right things with our diet, exercise, water intake, stretching, and appropriate mindset, our minds set on the Healer.

NOTE: The principles that I have taught works not only for healing but for ANY area that you are standing in faith about. Of course IF you believe that these things have ceased then nothing I am saying will make any sense to you. God HAS NOT ceased being the God of miracles and healing. He is just the same. Check out Phil Keaggy's song *Just The Same*.

CHAPTER TWELVE

FAITH CONCERNING HEALING

The name of this chapter is Faith Concerning Healing, however this thing called faith is not just for healing but for every area of our lives. The principles found within this chapter is what answered prayer is hinged upon. Read it, Read the Word,, study it, look up the recommended verses and answer the questions. I believe that as you do these things with the help of the Holy Spirit, that your mind will be renewed and you will begin to see through faith eyes whenever you are faced with anything. It is like this example: GODISNOWHERE. You will either see God is NO where or God is NOW here. It all depends on how you look at it. One is seen through the eyes of and mind not renewed by the Word which is of doubt and a mind that is renewed that sees through the eyes of faith.

> *"Faith comes by hearing and hearing concerning the Words concerning Christ (hearing an hearing the Word of God."*
>
> Romans 10:17

> *"Let him [If any man] (or her) who has ears to hear, let him/her hear."*
>
> Mark 4:9, 23, Revelation 2:7, 11, 17, 29

"Let him/her who has ears to hear, let him listen up and understand."

Mark 9, 23, Revelation 2:7, 11, 17, 29
with emphasis and addition mine

This phrase about hearing occurs *7(seven) times.*

What does this have to do with healing? Everything!

Your ears are not just the flaps on the side of your noggin. They (the auricles/pinna) are merely collectors of sounds/words. As the sound/word goes from acoustic, to mechanical to hydraulic to neurological where the sound is transmitted to the brain and the receiver and transmitter responds back.

The sounds/words are "heard" and then processed where the sounds/words are understood.

Jesus wants us to hear and understand what is being said. This goes for faith coming by hearing and understands concerning the Word of God and in our case the, Word of God, concerning *healing.*

There are *many voices* speaking many *things* concerning *healing.* Some are in denial that it is the *WILL OF GOD ON EARTH AS IT IS IN HEAVEN* (*yes, capitalization for the purpose of you hearing*) for you to be *healed.*

This is the reason that I keep on writing these things concerning *healing.*

IF you are filled with doubt, unbelief, fear, and you are vacillating (alternate or waver between different opinions or actions; be indecisive) between being sick or healed, then you may need to have an ear examination and determine what you are allowing in your spiritual and physical hearing mechanisms. You may need to have your ears (between the flaps on your noggin to the tympanic membrane (a membrane forming part of the organ of hearing, which vibrates in response to sound waves. In humans and other higher vertebrates it forms the eardrum, between the outer and middle ear) cleaned out by the removal of cerumen (ear wax) or a hearing aid to facilitate the loss of hearing by nerve damage.

OR you may just need to *"listen up."*

Of course the primary reason for this chapter (and book) is concerning faith for healing, but again we need to understand that faith touches every area of our lives and the principles that are being outlined in this book applies. So let us take a look at this thing called faith. I will use The Amplified Bible on the various verses about faith.

The first place to start is the Biblical definition of faith.

HEBREWS 11: 1

> *"Now faith is the assurance (the confirmation, the title deed) of the things [we] hope for, being the proof of things we do not see and the conviction of their reality [faith perceiving as real fact what is not revealed to the senses].*
>
> Hebrews 11:1, AMP

The word assurance is the substance, something that is tangible.

SUBSTANCE: hupostasis (hoop-os'-tas-is)= a *setting under* (*support*), that is, (figuratively) concretely *essence*, or abstractly *assurance* (objectively or subjectively): - confidence, confident, person, substance.

This thing called faith is not just some ethereal non-tangible experience. We have an assurance where we know that we know that we know that the Lord's Word is not only truth but is also reality. When we are faced with sickness we know that we know that we know that the will of God is healing on earth as it is in heaven. There is a confirmation that backs up what we hear from the Word. I like the idea of a title deed of ownership. When you buy a piece of land, I don't have to go down to the land every day to make sure it is mine. I know it is mine because of the document I have in hand. The same with faith, I know that healing is mine because I have the Word of God in hand that says it is so.

Faith is the substance of things hoped for.

THINGS: pragma (prag'-mah):= a *deed*; by implication an *affair*; by extension an *object* (material): - business, matter, thing, work.

HOPED FOR: elpizō (el-pid'-zo)=From G1680; to *expect* or *confide:* - (have, thing) hope (-d) (for), trust. G1680: elpis (el-pece')=From elpō which is a primary word (to *anticipate*, usually with pleasure); *expectation* (abstract or concrete) or *confidence:* - faith, hope.

The bottom line is that when you have faith you have a confident expectation that what you are standing in faith is yours. Not just going to be yours but is at that moment yours.

EVIDENCE: elegchos (el'-eng-khos)=From G1651; *proof, conviction:* - evidence, reproof. G1651: elegchō (el-eng'-kho)=Of uncertain affinity; to *confute, admonish:* - convict, convince, tell a fault, rebuke, reprove.

If our faith was put on trial, there would be evidence, proof, that what we were believing was real.

THING NOT SEEN: blepō (blep'-o)=A primary verb; to *look* at (literally or figuratively): - behold, beware, lie, look (on, to), perceive, regard, see, sight, take heed.

When we pray for healing, there may or may not be an immediate manifestation of the healing, but if there is no manifestation by faith when we look at the situation, we see through eyes of faith and see the healing.

We have all the evidence we need because we believe the Word of God. Our convictions are based not on what we see in the physical but by what we believe in the spiritual. In The Amplified Bible it says "faith perceiving as real fact what is not revealed to the senses."

It has been said (by whom I don't know), "When truth is blurred by lies and misinformation, perception becomes reality and all is lost." What people perceive is usually what they believe, and this is based on what they hear, see and think."

Our perception in faith is not based on what we see, hear, feel or think, but on the Word of God "faith perceiving as real fact what is not revealed to the senses."

HOMEWORK

1. What is the first thing that faith is? (Hebrews 11:1)
2. What is the relationship between the substance and hope (Hebrews 11:1)

CLUE: Tangible things.

NOTE: Remember that hope means "confident expectation.

3. What do you think things are?

4. What is faith evidence? (Hebrews 11:1)

NOTE: Again, tangible things is rooted in hope and faith. Tangible things can be anything that you are standing for in faith including physical, tangible healing of your body.

5. Is this faith evidence visual? (Hebrews 11:1)

6. If this faith evidence is not visible to the naked eye, what is it?

NOTE: If it can be seen then you do not need faith. By faith we perceive as real fact what is not revealed to the senses.

In our next chapter we will look at how to walk (regulate ourselves and conduct our lives) by faith and not by sight in II Corinthians 5:7.

CHAPTER THIRTEEN

FAITH FOR REGULATION AND CONDUCT

"Have faith in God, constantly…for we walk by faith [we regulate our lives and conduct ourselves, on the assurance (substance, the confirmation, the title deed] of things we] hope for (confident expectation) the proof/evidence of things we do not see and the conviction of their reality faith perceiving as real fact what is not revealed to the senses."
Mark 11:22, II Corinthians 5:7, Hebrews 11:1, AMP
with emphasis and additions mine

This thing called faith is not just a whim, or passing fancy, or something that we need when we are in dire straits. Faith is a lifestyle as we live by faith (Romans 1:17), it is a walk as we regulate our lives and conduct ourselves not only daily but 24/7/365 which means 24 hours in a day, seven days a week, and 365 days out of the year—not just on Sundays.

This timeframe of faith will become invaluable as you are standing in faith for a healing. If it is not an immediate healing, it may drag on for days or years, so you will need the ability to not walk by reality (what you see) but will need to walk in truth (The Word of God, John 17:17)

We do not deny reality because reality is, well, real. We

don't deny a diagnosis from a physician because they work with what they know, with what they see, with test results and bodily functions. But we do draw the line for accepting a prognosis, their professional opinion based on reality. When we see or hear about reality, then we trump reality with truth.

"Sanctify them by truth, Thy Word is truth."

John 17:17

Mark 11:22 is a response by Jesus to the boys (His disciples) when they noticed that the fig tree that He had spoken to (cursed) was withered from the roots up to the leaves. Jesus takes the opportunity to teach on how to pray with continual faith the Word of God.

Jesus was coming into Jerusalem and He had sent two of His disciples into a village to find a colt (donkey) so He could ride into Jerusalem. (Mark 11:1-7) As He approached Jerusalem there was a procession of His followers going before Him and the colt, and they were spreading their coats in the road along with leafy branches from the fields. They were not religious and somber but they were SHOUTING loudly.

"HOSANNA IN THE HIGHTEST! BLESSED IS HE WHO COME IN THE NAME OF THE LORD; BLESSED IS THE COMING KINGDOM OF OUR FATHER DAVID; HOSANNA IN THE HIGHEST!"
Mark 11:9-10, Zechariah 9:9, Psalm 118:26

These words are in capital letters and boldly highlight to show the intensity of this procession into Jerusalem.

HOSANNA: hōsanna (ho-san-nah')= *oh save!*; *hosanna* (that is, *hoshia-na*), an exclamation of adoration: - hosanna.

BLESSED: eulogeō (yoo-log-eh'-o) = From a compound of G2095 and G3056; to *speak well of*, that is, (religiously) to *bless* (*thank* or *invoke a benediction upon, prosper*): - bless, praise.

THE RECONNISANCE MISSION

Jesus enters Jerusalem and scopes out the temple. He looked around at all the activity that was taking place and then He left for Bethany with the twelve (Peter, Andrew, James, John, Philip, Thaddeus, Bartholomew, Thomas, James Simon, Matthew, Judas). The reason for leaving Jerusalem and onward to Bethany is because it was "already late". (Mark 11:11)

On the next day the group left for Bethany. Jesus (being the human that He was although He was God in the flesh, John 1:1-14) became hungry. He saw from a distance a fig tree that was in leaf.

NOTE: Normally the fruit and leaves appear at the same time.

"Fig Tree Will Not Fruit Because of Watering Conditions. If a fig tree is suffering from water stress caused by either too little or too much water, this can cause it to stop producing figs or never start producing, especially if it is a younger tree." (www.gardeningknowhow.com)

The reason for the tree to only have leaves and no figs was due to the fact that it was not the season for figs. (Mark 11:13) Jesus went to check it out (1) because He was hungry (2) Perhaps [perhaps not] He would find "anything on it" which He did not.

Jesus began to speak to the inanimate object called the fig tree. There is no indication that Jesus was throwing a fit or angry, but He did speak to the tree because there was no figs.

"He said to it (the fig tree), may no one ever eat fruit from you again!"

Mark 11:13

The exclamation mark at the end of the sentence speaks of the passion with which Jesus spoke. As Jesus spoke to the inanimate fig tree, His disciples were listening. (Mark 11:14) In my imagination I can see the disciples listening, looking at one another wondering about why the one that they were following was talking to a tree. Of course, over the course of time they had been with Him they had seen many strange and unexplainable things.

They continued on to Jerusalem, entered the temple and Jesus began to drive out those who were buying and selling in the temple and began to turn over the tables of the money changers and the seats of those who were selling doves, and then He would not permit anyone to carry merchandise through the temple. (Mark 11:15-16)

NOTE: The sacrifices that were to be made to Lord must be without blemish. The sellers had animals for sale for sacrifice. Many who came to Jerusalem came from far away and did not have animals so they had to purchase from the sellers. They did not have anytime tellers, so there were people there were tables of the money changers to exchange Greek and Roman coins into "the standard shekel" that they could then in turn buy the sacrifice needed. (Note from Ryrie Study Bible) "The merchants were guilty of profanation of the Temple and of excess profiteering." (Ryrie Study Bible note on Mark 11:15)

NOTE: Some people equate this to people selling merchandise in a church service. I don't think so. (1) They were not selling anything that could access God (2) They sell product not privilege for access into His presence. Sometimes it has been said by many that the animals that they sold were with blemish so useless for sacrifice.

Jesus began to teach them. Of course in our modern day church we like to start off the message with a joke to lighten up the room, but Jesus chose to cause trouble before He taught.

> "Is it not written (in Isaiah 56:7, Jeremiah 7:11) 'My house shall be called a house of prayer for all the nations? But you have made it a robbers den.'"
>
> Mark 11: 17
> addition mine

NOTE: It seems to me that this was a pretty short teaching. I know that when I started preaching/teaching when I first got saved, that my message lasted maybe five minutes, and now I can go on for 45 minutes or more.

NOTE TO THE NOTE: I don't think there is a time limit as many of Jesus' teachings and parables were quite lengthy.

The religious leaders (chief priests and the scribes) heard what Jesus had said and the cause and effect was that they "began seeking how to destroy Him." (Mark 11:18) The reason for this was because, "they were afraid of Him." (Mark 11:18) The whole crowd was astonished that this man had come in and disrupted the house because of His teaching. (Mark 11:18)

Evening came (he had been there since morning) and they left Jerusalem to go back to Bethany. The thing that started with a recon mission was now completed, mission accomplished. (Mark 11:19)

On the returned trip to Bethany, it was morning (they left Jerusalem in the evening and when they arrived it was morning), they came upon the same fig tree that Jesus spoke to. What once was a leafy green tree with no figs was now a tree that was withered from the roots up. Apparently what Jesus had spoken to the tree came to pass. Peter's memory was triggered as he saw the fig tree. (Mark 11:20:21) He pointed out to Jesus (the obvious) "Rabbi, look the fig tree which you cursed (spoke to) has withered." (Mark 11:21)

Jesus' response was so simple yet so profound.

"Have faith in God, constantly."

Mark 11:22, AMP

Jesus then used this as an opportunity on how to pray with constant faith. He had just declared to the people in Jerusalem about how the house of prayer had turned into a den of thieves, (Mark 11:17) and now He was teaching the boys how to pray properly with faith.

HOMEWORK

"Have faith in God, constantly (7/24/365)"

Mark 11:22, AMP
with addition mine

1. How often should you have this thing called faith?

120

2.   Who is this faith to be in? (Mark 11:22, AMP)

*"For we walk by faith [we] regulate our lives and con-
duct ourselves by our conviction or belief respecting man's
relationship to God and divine things, with trust and holy
fervor; thus we walk] not by sight or appearance."*
                                       II Corinthians 5:7, AMP

3.   How are we to walk (7/24/365)? (II Corinthians 5:7,
     AMP)
4.   What two things does walk by faith mean? (II Cor-
     inthians 5:7, AMP)
5.   What is this regulation and conduct based upon? (II
     Corinthians 5:7, AMP)
6.   What two things are this faith walk in respective of?
     (II Corinthians 5:7, AMP)
7.   What do we do with our conviction and belief in rela-
     tion to God and divine things? (II Corinthians 5:7,
     AMP)
8.   What two things do we not walk by? (II Corinthians
     5:7, AMP)

*"Truly I say to you, whoever says to this mountain, 'be
taken up and cast into the sea,' and does not doubt in his
heart but believes that what he says is going to happen , it
will be granted."*
                                                   Mark 11:23

9.   When you have "faith in God, constantly" where is
     this faith manifested? (Mark 11:23)
10. What inanimate object are you to speak to? (Mark 11:23)

121

11. What two things are we to speak by constant faith to the mountain and tell the mountain what to do? (Mark 11:23)

NOTE: In my mind I am thinking that the mountain is representative of anything that is standing in our way.

12. What are we not to do and what are we to do when we speak to the mountain? (Mark 11:23)

13. Where does the belief take place? (Mark 11:23)

NOTE: Believe means to (1) trust in (2) cling to (3) rely on (4) adhere to according to John 3:16, AMP.

14. What are you believing? (Mark 11:23)

NOTE: Your words are reflective of what is in your heart manifest in what you say, your speech.

15. What is the cause and effect of praying/speaking this way?

"Therefore (what Jesus just taught) I say to you, all things for which you pray and ask, believe that you have received them, and thy will be granted you."

Mark 11:24

16. How many things are covered in this prayer/speaking to the mountain? (Mark 11:24

17. What are the three aspects mentioned in connection with this prayer of constant faith? (Mark 11:24)

18. When you pray, ask and believe, what is the time frame of the answer/granted prayer? (Mark 11:24)

19. What is the cause and effect of praying, asking and believing that you "have received" them before the actual manifestation? (Mark 11:24)

"Whenever you stand praying, forgive, if you have any-thing against anyone, so that your Father who is in heaven will also forgive you your transgressions."

Mark 11:25

NOTE: The word "whenever" implies that it is not just a one-time prayer it is "whenever."

20. What words speaks of the tenacity of prayer and not just a posture in prayer? (Mark 11:25)

NOTE: Standing is also used in our struggle against the true enemy (the d-evil) and not against flesh and blood. The word is part of resisting the enemy. (See Ephesians 6:10-18)

21. What are you to do as you stand in constant faith in prayer? (Mark 11:25)

22. What is the Triple AAA method of forgiving? (Mark 11:25)

"And whenever you stand praying, if you have anything against anyone, forgive him and let it drop, leave it, let it go, in order that your Father Who is in heaven may also forgive you your [own] failings and shortcomings and let them drop."

Mark 11:25, AMP

NOTE: The Triple AAA method of forgiveness
A= anything
A= against
A= anyone

This covers every possible scenario of offense and treachery against you. Of course anything that you have been through does NOT compare to anything that you have been through.

23. How is forgiveness (and your actions of forgiving)
    defined in the Amplified Bible)

FORGIVE

1. Let it drop (and don't pick it up again)
2. Leave it (leave it alone whenever it raises its ugly head)
3. Let it go (don't call it back after it goes)
4. Why forgive? (Mark 11:25, AMP)

CHAPTER FOURTEEN

ISAIAH 53:5-6
SIN OR SICKNESS OR BOTH

HEALED: râphâ' râphâh (raw-faw', raw-faw')=A primitive root; properly to mend (by stitching), that is, (figuratively) to cure: - cure, (cause to) heal, physician, repair, X thoroughly, make whole. H7503= râphâh (raw-faw') = A primitive root; to slacken (in many applications, literally or figuratively): - abate, cease, consume, draw [toward evening], fail, (be) faint, be (wax) feeble, forsake, idle, leave, let alone (go, down), (be) slack, stay, be still, be slothful, (be) weak (-en).

> *"Surely our griefs He Himself bore, and our sorrows He carried; yet we ourselves esteemed Him stricken, smitten of God, and afflicted. But He was pierced through for our transgressions, He was crushed for our iniquities; the chastening for our well-being fell upon Him, and by His scourging we are healed."*
>
> Isaiah 53:8

NOTE: The suffering Messiah pointing to Jesus and His D.B.R., Death Burial, Resurrection.

"Surely He has borne our griefs (sicknesses, weaknesses, and distresses) and carried our sorrows and pains [of punishment], yet we [ignorantly] considered Him stricken, smitten, and afflicted by God [as if with leprosy] but He was wounded for our transgressions, He was bruised for our guilt and iniquities; the chastisement [needful to obtain] peace and well-being for us was upon Him, and with the stripes [that wounded] Him the guilt and iniquity of us all."

Isaiah 53:4-5, AMP

M any theologians and lay minsters tend to say that this passage in Isaiah is only related to "sin sickness" and not "physical sickness." I get it, I know from where they are coming, but (however) I think they are wrong.

I believe that sickness is harassment and oppression from the d-evil that is rooted in sin/death/disobedience/a curse. (Acts 10:38, Genesis 2:16-17, Genesis 3:12-19, Romans 6:23)

Jesus came for the purpose of destroying the works of the d-evil (I John 3:8) For three years Jesus demonstrated the will of God on earth as it is in heaven (Acts 10:38) and culminated on the cross and resurrection, as He hung on a tree, became a curse in our place as He redeemed us from the curse of the law and healed all who were being harassed and oppressed by the d-evil so blessings of Abraham would come on us and the reception of the promise of the Spirit. (I Corinthians 15: 1-5, Galatians 3:13-14, Acts 10:38)

The Isaiah 53:4-5 verse is quoted 2 times in the New Testament. In the Matthew 8:17 verse, that healing is linked to the fulfillment of Isaiah 53:4-5, "by His stripes we were *healed.*"

"This was to fulfill what was spoken through Isaiah the prophet:
"He himself took our infirmities and carried away our diseases."
Matthew 8:17

INFIRMITIES: astheneia (as-then'-i-ah)=From G772 feebleness (of body or mind); by implication malady; moral frailty: - disease, infirmity, sickness, weakness. G772= asthenēs (as-then-ace')=strengthless (in various applications, literally, or figuratively and morally): - more feeble, impotent, sick, without strength, weak (-er, -ness, thing).

SICKNESS/DISEASE: nosos (nos'-os)=Of uncertain affinity; a malady (rarely figurative of moral disability): - disease, infirmity, sickness.

The context of Matthew 8:17 was not mankind's sin but the cause and effect of sin which was infirmity, sickness, manifested as harassment and oppression by the d-evil.

(Acts 10:38) The context was Peter's mother-in-law who was laying ill with a fever. Jesus touched her hand and the fever left her, and she got up and began waiting on him.

(Matthew 8:14-15) Later on that evening, many were brought to Him who were under the power of demons (not God) and Jesus drove out the spirits with a word and He *restored to health all who were sick.* (Matthew 8:16)

I am convinced that God's will on earth as it is in heaven for us is healing. (Matthew 6:10, Acts 10:38)

"Thy kingdom (rule, reign, foundation of power) come
(from headquarters in heaven), Thy will (wish, desire) be
done (accomplished and manifested) on earth (where there

is sin, sickness, dis-ease, dis-comfort, dys-function) as it is (the blueprint in heaven) in heaven (where there is no sickness, disease, cancer, diabetes, arthritis, etc.).

Matthew 6:10
with emphasis and addition mine

When I write things like this on Facebook in Healing 101 (a group of praying people believing in healing) and in this book (*On Earth As It is In Heaven*) I am under attack in my mind and body. The lies come that what I teach is not true, I can't even heal myself or loved ones. I take captive every thought and imagination that raises its ugly head against the knowledge of God. (II Corinthians 10:3-7)

HOMEWORK

"Surely He has borne (bears) our griefs (sicknesses, weaknesses, and distresses) and carried our sorrow and pains [of punishment], yet we [ignorantly] considered Him stricken, smitten, and afflicted by God [as with leprosy]."

Isaiah 53:4, AMP

1. When it says that He has born our griefs, what is included in our griefs? (Isaiah 53:4, AMP)
2. What did He carry? (Isaiah 53:4, AMP)
3. What is sorrows and pains considered to be? (Isaiah 53:4, AMP)

NOTE: Sorrows and pains are not a blessing but a curse of punishment. Jesus came to set us free of punishment.

4. Who did we ignorantly consider Jesus to be stricken, smitten and afflicted by? (Isaiah 53:4, AMP)

128

NOTE: So many times we believe that the sickness, disease. dis-comfort, and dysfuntion that we are stricken, smitten and afflicted by as coming from God. It is not from God but from the d-evil. This thought is ignorant.

"But (in contrast to Isaiah 53:4) he (Jesus) was wounded for our transgressions, He was bruised for our guilt and iniquities; the chastisement [needful to obtain] peace and well-being for us was upon Him, and with the stripes [that wounded] Him we are healed and made whole."

Isaiah 53:5

5. Why was He wounded? (Isaiah 53:5, AMP)
6. Why was He bruised? (Isaiah 53:5, AMP)
7. Why was His chastisement needful? (Isaiah 53:5, AMP)
8. By what were we healed and made whole? (Isaiah 53:5, AMP)

"All of us like sheep have gone astray, each of us has turned to his own way; but the Lord has caused the iniquity of us all to fall on Him."

Isaiah 53:6

9. What have we all done? (Isaiah 53:6)
10. What was our going astray like? (Isaiah 53:6)
11. What has each of us turned to? (Isaiah 53:6)
12. What has the Lord caused to happen? (Isaiah 53:6)
13. Where has the iniquity of us all fallen? (Isaiah 53:6)

NOTE: Isaiah 53:4-6 has been interpreted by many theologians to mean only "sin sickness." Many other theologians declare that healings, miracles, gifts of the Spirit have passed away when (1) the last apostle died (2) the church was established in Acts 2 (3) the canon (collected works of the Bible) were collected. I have no problem with Isaiah 53:4-6 referring to the work of the cross for our sins. As the song implied, He really did pay a debt that we owed as sinners, and yes He did pay the debt by the Death, Burial, and Resurrection on the cross but it is very clear to me that there was a dual purpose of the cross to deal with sins, poverty and sickness in our lives.

NOTE: There were two other places that refers to Isaiah 53:4 in the New Testament, Matthew 8:14-17, I Peter 2:24-25)

"And when Jesus went into Peter's house, He saw his mother-in-law lying ill with a fever. He touched her hand and the fever left her; and she got up and began waiting on Him. When evening came, they brought to Him many who were under the power of demons, and He drove out the spirits with a word and restored to health all who were sick. And this He fulfilled what was spoken by the prophet Isaiah, He Himself took [in order to carry away] our weaknesses and infirmities and bore away our diseases."

Matthew 8:14-17, Isaiah 53:4, AMP

14. Whose house did Jesus go into? (Matthew 8:14, AMP)
15. Who did Jesus see when He entered the house? (Matthew 8:14, AMP)
16. What was wrong with Peter's mother-in-law? (Matthew 8:14, AMP)

NOTE: She was not lying with sin but she was lying ill with sickness.

17. What was Peter's mother-in-law lying ill with? (Matthew 8:14, AMP)

130

18. What did Jesus touch? (Matthew 8:115, AMP)

NOTE: In the Gospels, there were around ten different methods of Jesus' healing including, speaking, touching, spit mud in the eyes, fingers in the ears, etc. This is akin to the "gifts (plural) of healing" and "the effecting of miracles" (plural) found in I Corinthians 12:8-10). To me this is part of "the works that I do, he will do also; and greater works than theses he will do; because I go to the Father."(John 14:12-13) In the case of Peter's mother-in-law He just touched here and the fever left.

19. What three things happened when Jesus touched her? (Matthew 8:14, AMP).

20. Who was brought to Jesus at Peter's mother-in-law's house that evening? (Matthew 8:15, AMP).

21. What was the people's problem that was brought to Jesus? (Matthew 8:15, AMP)

22. How did Jesus deal with those who were brought to Him? (Matthew 8:15, AMP).

23. What was the quantity of people brought to Jesus? (Matthew 8:15, AMP)

24. What was the cause and effect of Jesus casting out the spirits with a word? (Matthew 8:18, AMP)

25. How many were healed of being ill? (Matthew 8:18)

NOTE: In this case the illness was related to spirits, demon possession. Manifestation of this demon-possession was sickness (not just sin).

"He sends forth His word and heals them and rescues them from the pit and destruction."

Psalm 107:20

26. What was these healings, Peter's mother-in-law's fever and those demon-possessed, who were healed a fulfillment of? (Matthew 8:17, Isaiah 53:4)

NOTE: So this event of the cross by which people were healed by His stripes was not limited to "spiritual sickness" but also for "physical sickness".

CHAPTER FIFTEEN

THE BENEFITS PACKAGE

"Bless the Lord, O my soul, and all that is within me, bless His holy name. Bless the Lord, O my soul and forget none of His benefits"

Psalm 103:1, 2

"Bless (affectionately, gratefully praise) the Lord, O my soul; and all that is [deepest] within me, bless His holy name! Bless (affectionately, gratefully praise) the Lord, O my soul, and forget no [one of His benefits."

Psalm 103:1-2, AMP

BLESSED: bârak (baw-rak')=A primitive root; to kneel; by implication to bless God (as an act of adoration), and (vice-versa) man (as a benefit); also (by euphemism) to curse (God or the king, as treason): - X abundantly, X altogether, X at all, blaspheme, bless, congratulate, curse, X greatly, X indeed, kneel (down), praise, salute, X still, thank.

"Bless the Lord= Adore and thank Him for all benefits."
(Ryrie Study Bible note on Psalm 103:1)

SOUL: nephesh (neh'-fesh)=From H5314; properly a breathing creature, that is, animal or (abstractly) vitality; used very widely in a literal, accommodated or figurative sense (bodily or mental): - any, appetite, beast, body, breath, creature, X dead (-ly), desire, X [dis-] contented, X fish, ghost, + greedy, he, heart (-y), (hath, X jeopardy of) life (X in jeopardy), lust, man, me, mind, mortality, one, own, person, pleasure, (her-, him-, my-, thy-) self, them (your) -selves, + slay, soul, + tablet, they, thing, (X she) will, X would have it. 5314: nâphash (naw-fash'= A primitive root; to breathe; passively, to be breathed upon, that is, (figuratively) refreshed (as if by a current of air): - (be) refresh selves (-ed).

One command to the soul to bless the Lord is enough, but to get the importance of "blessing the Lord" means it is really, really, really important.

You would think that we would remember to bless the Lord and not to forget His benefits, but as we live out our lives we tend to get to busy, distracted and weary. Just like our physical bodies get tired and forget, so it is with our souls.

BENEFITS: gemûl (ghem-ool)'=From H1580; treatment, that is, an act (of good or ill); by implication service or requital: - + as hast served, benefit, desert, deserving, that which he hath given, recompence, reward. H1580: gâmal (gaw-mal')=A primitive root; to treat a person (well or ill), that is, benefit or requite; by implication (of toil) to ripen, that is, (specifically) to wean: - bestow on, deal bountifully, do (good), recompense, requite, reward, ripen, + serve, wean, yield.

As a Speech-Language Pathologist, I work with Speech, Dysphagia (swallowing disorders) and Cognitive Issues (including memory). For more information on this check out my book, *Speaking and Hearing the Word of God: A Speech-Language Pathologist's Perspective.*

I like to call the Blessings, His Benefits Package. In our business world we look for what the company benefits are including money, insurance, 401K, retirement benefits. God has a Benefits Package that we sometimes forget when we grow weary as we work in the Kingdom, so we need to remember and not forget what God has for us, not only in the sweet bye and bye but in the nitty gritty now and now.

BENEFITS PACKAGE

1. Pardons ALL your iniquities
2. Heals ALL your diseases
3. Redeems your life from the pit
4. Crowns you with lovingkindness (love) and compassion (mercy)
5. Satisfies your years with good things (not bad things)
6. Your youth is renewed like the eagle

NOTE: These are the first six benefits but verses 6-22 lists many more.

HOMEWORK

1. What does the Lord pardon? (Psalm 103:3)
2. How many of our iniquities does He pardon? (Psalm 103:3)

PARDONS: sâlach (saw-lakh')= A primitive root; to forgive: - forgive, pardon, spare.

INIQUITIES: aw-vone', (aw-vone')= From perversity, that is, (moral) evil: - fault, iniquity, mischief, punishment (of iniquity), sin.

NOTE: The pardon comes from headquarters (heaven) and was manifested on earth, on the cross (Death, Burial, Resurrection) of Jesus. This is for every human being who ever lived and died but is hinged on *if* they believe (trust in, cling to, rely on, adhere to) in God's only begotten Son (Jesus). (See John 3:16)

3. What does the Lord do with all your diseases? (Psalm 103:3)

HEALS: râphâ' râphâh (raw-faw', raw-faw')=A primitive root; properly to mend (by stitching), that is, (figuratively) to cure: - cure, (cause to) heal, physician, repair, X thoroughly, make whole.

4. How many of your diseases does He heal? (Psalm 103:3)

ALL: kôl kôl (kole, kole)= From H3634; properly the whole; hence all, any or every (in the singular only, but often in a plural sense): - (in) all (manner, [ye]), altogether, any (manner), enough, every (one, place, thing), howsoever, as many as, [no-] thing, ought, whatsoever, (the) whole, whoso (-ever). H3634: kâlal (kaw-lal')= A primitive root; to complete: - (make) perfect.

DISEASE (DIS-EASE) tachălû' tachălû' (takh-al-oo', takh-al-oo')= From H2456; a malady: - disease, X grievous, (that are) sick (-ness). H2456: châlâ' (khaw-law')= A primitive root (compare H2470); to be sick: - be diseased.

136

NOTE: As of 2018 there are here are about 100,000 human diseases that have been identified in this World. There are approximately 80 different types of autoimmune diseases.

5.   From what does He redeem your life? (Psalm 103:4)

REDEEM: gâ'al (gaw-al')=A primitive root, to redeem (according to the Oriental law of kinship), that is, to be the next of kin (and as such to buy back a relative's property, marry his widow, etc.): - X in any wise, X at all, avenger, deliver, (do, perform the part of near, next) kinsfolk (-man), purchase, ransom, redeem (-er), revenger.

6.   What does He crown you with? (Psalm 103: 4)

CROWNS: aw-tar' = A primitive root; to encircle (for attack or protection); especially to crown (literally or figuratively): - compass, crown.

LOVING KINDNESS: chêsêd (kheh'-sed)=From H2616; kindness; by implication (towards God) piety; rarely (by opprobrium) reproof, or (subjectively) beauty: - favour, good deed (-liness, -ness), kindly, (loving-) kindness, merciful (kindness), mercy, pity, reproach, wicked thing.

COMPASSION/TENDER MERCIES: racham (rakh'-am) =From H7355; compassion (in the plural); by extension the womb (as cherishing the foetus); by implication a maiden: - bowels, compassion, damsel, tender love, (great, tender) mercy, pity, womb. H7355: râcham (raw-kham') = A primitive root; to fondle; by implication to love, especially to compassionate:

- have compassion (on, upon), love, (find, have, obtain, shew) mercy (-iful, on, upon), (have) pity, Ruhamah, X surely.

7. What does the Lord do with your years? (Psalm 103:5)

SATISFIES: saw-bah', saw-bay'-ah =A primitive root; to sate, that is, fill to satisfaction (literally or figuratively): - have enough, fill (full, self, with), be (to the) full (of), have plenty of, be satiate, satisfy (with), suffice, be weary of.

NOTE: In the 60's The Rolling Stones lamented that they could not get "no" satisfaction. The counterpoint from the Jesus Movement (hippies who accept Jesus) was, yes you can!

8. What does the Lord use to satisfy your years? (Psalm 103:5)

GOOD (things) tobe = From H2895; good (as an adjective) in the widest sense; used likewise as a noun, both in the masculine and the feminine, the singular and the plural (good, a good or good thing, a good man or woman; the good, goods or good things, good men or women), also as an adverb (well): - beautiful, best, better, bountiful, cheerful, at ease, X fair (word), (be in) favour, fine, glad, good (deed, -lier, liest, -ly, -ness, -s), graciously, joyful, kindly, kindness, liketh (best), loving, merry, X most, pleasant, + pleaseth, pleasure, precious, prosperity, ready, sweet, wealth, welfare, (be) well ([-favoured]). H2895: tobe =A primitive root, to be (transitively do or make) good (or well) in the widest sense: - be (do) better, cheer, be (do, seem) good, (make), goodly, X please, (be, do, go, play) well.

NOTE: Things are not bad, otherwise the Lord would not use "things" to satisfy us. The things that He uses so we can have satisfaction are "good things."

CHAPTER SIXTEEN

THE PURPOSE OF JESUS
THE HEALER ON THE MOVE AND HE IS STILL ON THE MOVE.

For the rest the book, we will be looking at Jesus in the Gospels (the good news about the death, burial and resurrection, and the cause and effect as he went about, doing good, and healing all who were oppressed and harassed by the d-evil for God was with Him (Immanuel, God with us).

"...the reason the Son of God was made manifest (visible) was to undo (destroy, loosen, and dissolve) the works the d-evil has done."

I John 3:8, AMP
addition mine

"And He went about all Galilee, teaching in their synagogues and preaching the good news (Gospel) of the Kingdom (rule, reign, foundation of power) and healing every disease and every weakness and infirmity among the people."

Matthew 4:23
with emphasis and additions mine

NOTE: Matthew 4:23 is Jesus' modus operandi (M.O.)

"(You Know) how God anointed and consecrated Jesus of Nazareth with the [Holy] Spirit and with strength and ability and power (duNAmis, dynamic ability); how He went about doing good and, in particular, curing all who were harassed and oppressed by [the power of] the d-evil, for God was with Him."

Acts 10:38, AMP
with emphasis and additions mine

NOTE: Jesus the manifested will of God (God in the flesh, John 1:1-14) who went about and doing good (not bad) for three years demonstrating God's will on earth as it is in heaven. (Matthew 6:10)

NOTE: Acts 10:38 and Matthew 6:10 are the foundations for this book.

In the Gospels we see that there are 41 incidences of healing where Jesus utilized 10 methods to facilitate the healings.

Thanx and a Tip O Da Hat to John Wimber and Kevin Springer for gleaned insights on healing from the book *Power Healing*, Harper and Row, Publishers, San Francisco 1987.

1. Drove out demons
2. Word spoken
3. Touched by Jesus
4. Prayer of another
5. Faith of another
6. Preaching of Jesus
7. The person's faith
8. Jesus moved by compassion
9. Person touches Jesus
10. Teaching of Jesus

NOTE: While we have covered of a few of these incidences in previous chapters, we will go over them again along with the complete listing of the 41 healings. I have placed what happened and the verses where the healing took place. I will usually only use the first Scripture listed. The others can be yours to use for further study.

HOMEWORK/WORKBOOK

#1 THE MAN WITH AN UNCLEAN SPIRIT (Mark 1:23-25, Luke 4: 31-37)

I hope that by now you have seen that it is the will of God to heal the sick. In Psalm 107:20 we see that Jesus sent His word (Jesus=the Word=God in the flesh, John 1:1) to heal and deliver them. As we start off this section we see that Jesus is dealing with an unclean spirit.

"And He healed many who were ill with various diseases, and cast out many demons…"

Mark 1:37

1. Where was this man? (Mark 1:23)
2. What was the man's problem? (Mark 1:23)
3. What did the man do verbally? (Mark 1:23)
4. What did the demons say through the man? (Mark 1:24)
5. What did Jesus tell the demons to do? (Mark 1:24)

REBUKE: epitimaō (ep-ee-tee-mah'-o)= to tax upon, that is, censure or admonish; by implication forbid: - (straitly) charge, rebuke.

NOTE: I have heard Oral Roberts say that the word rebuke means, "Stop it, that's enough!"

6. What was the cause and effect of Jesus' rebuke? (Mark 1:26)
7. Did this event take place in private or in public? (Mark 1:27, Luke 4:35-36)

#2 PETER'S MOTHER-IN LAW (Matthew 8:14-15, Mark 1:30-31, Luke 4:38-39)

I like this healing because it shows me that God is not just concerned with the major sicknesses in our lives. He wants to touch us from fever to cancer. Also in this healing we see that Jesus did not touch the lady but merely touched her with no words.

1. Where did Jesus come into? (Matthew 8:14)
NOTE: Peter was married.
2. What did Jesus see? (Matthew 8:14)
3. What was wrong with Peter's mother-in-law? (Matthew 8:14)
4. What method did Jesus use to heal her? (Matthew 8:15)
5. What did the fever do? (Matthew 8:15)
6. What was the cause and effect of Peter's mother-in-law being healed? (Matthew 8:16)
7. When word got out, what did people do? (Matthew 8:16)
8. What was the condition of the people who were brought to Jesus? (Matthew 8:16)
9. What did Jesus do? (Matthew 8:16)
10. What method did Jesus use to deliver them? (Matthew 8:16)
11. While they were demon-possessed, what were they healed of? (Matthew 8:16)

12. What did these healings fulfill? (Matthew 8:17, Isaiah 53:4)

NOTE: For those who say that Isaiah 53 was only for salvation, I believe that this salvation includes, saving from sin, deliverance from demonic forces, and healing of the physical body.

#3 MULTITUDES #1 (Matthew 8:16-17, Mark 1:32-34, Luke 4:40)

Jesus was the master of the isolated incidence of healing one on one, however he gathered large crowds and healed them all (those who believed). In these 41 incidences of Jesus demonstrating the Kingdom of God on earth as it is in heaven this is #1 of 10 healings within multitudes.

1. Who had gathered at the door of Peter's mother-in-law's house? Were they a few or many? (Mark 1:33)
2. How many did He heal? (Mark 1:34)
3. What were people will with? (Mark 1:34)
4. What did Jesus cast out a He healed many? (Mark 1:34)
5. Did Jesus permit the demons to speak or carry on a running conversation with them? (Mark 1:34)

#4 MANY DEMONS (Mark 1:35-39)

Once again we see the demonic influence on sickness and disease and how Dr. Jesus diagnosed the problem and cut at the root of the sickness on many, demonic influence.

1. What did Jesus do early in the morning while it was still dark? (Mark 1:35)
2. Where did Jesus go when He left Peter's mother-in-law's house? (Mark 1:35

3. What did Jesus do when He reached a secluded? (Mark 1:35)
4. What did Peter and his companions do when they could not find Jesus? (Mark 1:36)
5. What did they say to Jesus when they found Him? (Mark 1:37)
6. What did Jesus want to do and why? (Mark 1:38)
7. Why did He say that He wanted to preach? (Mark 1:38)
8. Why did Jesus come to planet Earth? (I John 3:8)
9. When they went into the synagogues throughout all Galilee, what two things did He do? (Mark 1:39)

NOTE: Remember Jesus' modus operandi (M.O.) He went about (1) teaching in their synagogues (2) declaring the gospel (good news) of the Kingdom (3) healing the sick. (Matthew 4:22-25) Later on He would pass on the mission to His disciples and via them to us (Matthew 28:18-20, John 17:-21) to do the same works and even greater works. (John 14:11-14)

#5 LEPER (Matthew 8:2:4, Mark 1:40-42, Luke 5:13-13)

Leprosy was a skin disease that was considered to be a curse. In the Fat Part of the Book (aka the Old Testament there are specific rules and regulations on how to deal with the dis-ease. In cases of leprosy Jesus instructed them to go and present an offering to the priest. (See Leviticus 13-15 for full details) In Isaiah 53:4 we see that it was ignorantly believed that Jesus was stricken, smitten and afflicted by God (He did not do it) "as if with leprosy." (Isaiah 53:4, AMP)

1. Where did Jesus come down from? (Matthew 8:1)

NOTE: Jesus had been on the mountain presented the way, the principles of the Kingdom of God. As Bob Mumford puts it in his book, *The King and You*, Jesus laid out the preamble and constitution and the principles of the Kingdom of God on earth as it is in heaven.

2. Who came up to Him as He came down? (Matthew 8:2)

3. What posture did the leper take before Jesus? Matthew 8:22)

4. What did the leper call Jesus? (Matthew 8:2)

LORD: kurios (koo'-ree-os) =From kuros (supremacy); supreme in authority, that is, (as noun) controller; by implication Mr. (as a respectful title): - God, Lord, master, Sir.

Lord=
- Supremacy
- Supreme in authority (dominion)
- Controller, the one in control
- Mr. (respect)
- God
- Lord
- Master
- Sir

5. What did the leper want? (Matthew 1:2)

6. What caveat did the leper put on his cleansing? (Matthew 1:2)

IF THOU WILT: thelō tethelō (thel'-o, eth-el'-o) = that is, choose or prefer (literally or figuratively); by implication to wish, that is, be inclined to (sometimes adverbially gladly); impersonally for the future tense, to be about to; by Hebraism to delight in: - desire, be disposed (forward), intend, list, love, mean, please, have rather, (be) will (have, -ling, -ling [ly]).

NOTE: The root word for thelema (will, wish, desire). "Thy will (wish, desire, inclination) be done (accomplished or manifested) on earth as it is in heaven. On earth was leprosy, in heaven there is no leprosy. The leper wanted God's will on earth as it is in heaven which meant to remove the leprosy in his life.

7. What did Jesus say that he was? (Matthew 8:2)

NOTE: Jesus said concerning healing the leper that His will was God's will as I said, "I will."

8. What two methods did Jesus use to cleanse him of his leprosy? (Matthew 8:2)

9. As Jesus stretched out His hand and touch the leper, what two things did Jesus say? (Matthew 8:2)

10. How much time lapsed for the healing (leprosy cleansing) take place? (Matthew 8:2)

NOTE: According to Old Testament law (Leviticus 14:1-31) Jesus told the ex-leper to go to the priest (religious leader) and present the offering that Moses commanded, as a testimony to them.

According to the Ryrie Study Bible, no one had been cured of leprosy except Miriam (Numbers 12:10-15)

#6 PARALYTIC (Matthew 9:2-7, Mark 2:3-5, Luke 5:17-25)

We have seen Jesus healing people with demons, fever, leprosy and now the inability to move a man's paralyzed limbs. People had to bring him laying on a pallet by faith. In Isaiah 53:4-5 many people equate these verses with the healing of "spiritual sickness" but Jesus linked spiritual and physical healing to "by His stripes you were healed." In this passage we see Jesus pronouncing forgiveness of sins and then easily pronouncing physical healing as the man went from not being able to move his limbs to being able to moving his limbs.

1. Jesus came to Capernaum (his own city) by boat. Who did they bring to Him? (Matthew 9:2)
2. What was the condition of the man that they brought to Him? (Matthew 9:2)

PARALYTIC/PALSY: paralutikos (par-al-oo-tee-kos') = as if dissolved, that is, "paralytic": - that had (sick of) the palsy.

3. What position was the paralytic in? (Matthew 9:2)
4. What did Jesus see? (Matthew 9:2)

NOTE: The word "they" indicates that he saw the faith of those who brought the man to Him, but can also mean he saw the faith of the man also.

5. What did Jesus say to the paralytic? (Matthew 9:2)

NOTE: Jesus did not specifically address the spiritual condition of the man but spoke to the issue of sin, which He forgave.

6. What was the reaction of some of the scribes (religious leaders)? Matthew 9:3)
7. What did they say "this fellow" had done? (Matthew 9:3)

BLASPHEMES: blasphēmeō (blas-fay-meh'-o) =From G989; to vilify; specifically to speak impiously: - (speak)

148

blaspheme (-er, -mously, -my), defame, rail on, revile, speak evil.

8. How did "this fellow" blaspheme? (Matthew 9:2)
9. What did Jesus know? (Matthew 9:4)

NOTE: Jesus was not a mind reader with cheap parlor tricks or evil powers, but he did have a connection with the Holy Spirit who had words of knowledge.

10. What did Jesus ask the scribes? (Matthew 9:4)
11. Jesus posed a question to the scribes by giving the two options, what were the choses Jesus gave them? (Matthew 9:5)
12. What did Jesus give them so they would know that the Son of Man (has has authority on earth on earth? (Matthew 9:6)
13. What three things did the heled paralytic do? (Matthew 9:6)
14. What was the reaction of the crowds as they saw the paralytic man walking around? (Matthew 9:6)?
15. What did they glorify God about? (Matthew 9:6)

#7 MAN WITH A WITHERED HAND (Matthew 12:9-13, Mark 3:1-5, Luke 6:6-10)

When I hear of a withered hand, I think of the fig tree that Jesus spoke to, and over a short period of time the tree was withered from the root up. (Mark 11:20-21) It appears that the man's hand was withered (from the inside out). The manifestation like most diseases starts somewhere within the immune system and manifests itself on the outside.

1. Where did Jesus run into the man with a withered hand?

2. What was the man's physical condition? (Matthew 12:10)

WITHERED: xēros (xay-ros') =From the base (through the idea of scorching); arid; by implication shrunken, earth (as opposed to water): - dry, land, withered.

3. What question did the religious people ask Jesus? (Matthew 12:10)

4. Why did they ask Jesus this question? (Matthew 12:10)

NOTE: I have noticed many people who don't believe in healing will ask you questions not because they want to know the answer but because they want to trap you.

5. What question did Jesus ask them to answer their question? What did Jesus ask them about the Sabbath?

NOTE: The Pharisees had already confronted Jesus about His disciples picking grain and eating because they were hungry on the Sabbath. They began to question the legality of doing this on the Sabbath. The "law" was explicit about the Sabbath. (Deuteronomy 23:25, Exodus 20:20) Jesus responds by quoting the Word about David. (I Samuel 21:3-4) He gave another example about the priests in the temple breaking bread on the Sabbath. (I Chronicles 6:18, Isaiah 66:1-2) Jesus then told them something was greater than the temple. Jesus again quotes the Word concerning the greater, "I desire compassion, and not a sacrifice" (Hosea 6:6)

6. Who did Jesus say was the Lord of the Sabbath? (Matthew 12:8)

"Jesus said to them, "The Sabbath was made for man, and not man for the Sabbath."

Mark 2:27

7. What value did Jesus put on the man with the withered hand versus a sheep (fallen in a pit)? Matthew 12:11)
8. What did Jesus say about healing the man on the Sabbath? (Matthew 12:12)
9. What did Jesus tell the man with the withered hand to do? (Matthew 12:12)

NOTE: Sometimes when there is something physically that we can't do, we may need to do what we can by faith like stretching out a withered hand.

10. What was the cause and effect of the man obeying Jesus to stretch out his hand? (Matthew 12:13)

NOTE: The Pharisees (the religious leaders) were not overjoyed at the healing of the man's withered hand.

11. What did the Pharisees (the religious leaders) conspire to do against Jesus? (Matthew 12:14)

#8 MULTITUDES # 2 (Matthew 12:15-16, Mark 3:9-11)

1. What was Jesus aware of? (Matthew 12:14)
2. What did Jesus do with this awareness? (Matthew 12:15)
3. What did many do and what was the result of them doing this? (Matthew 12:15)
4. What was Jesus' warning to them? (Matthew 12:16)
5. What was the fulfillment of Jesus' warning? (Matthew 12:17

"Behold, My Servant whom I have chosen; My beloved in whom My soul is well-pleased; I will put My Spirit upon Him and He shall proclaim justice to the Gentiles. He will not quarrel, nor cry out; nor will anyone hear His voice in the streets, a battered reed He will not break off, and a

smoldering wick He will not put out, until He leads justice to victory. And in His name the Gentiles will hope."
Isaiah 41:1-3

NOTE: Once again the Pharisees were conspiring against Jesus (with the Herodians) as to how they might destroy Him. (Mark 3:6)

6. When Jesus withdrew to the sea with His disciples, who followed Him from Galilee, Judea, Idumea, beyond the Jordan, and the vicinity of Tyre and Sidon? (Mark 3:7)

NOTE: This was considered to be a great number of people who heard of all that He was doing and came to him, also known as a multitude. (Mark 3:8)

7. What did Jesus tell his disciples? (Mark 3:9)
8. Why did Jesus tell them this? (Mark 3:9)
9. What had Jesus done for many? (Mark 3:10)
10. What was the result of Jesus healing many? (Mark 3:10)
11. Who pressed around Him in order that He would touch them? (Mark 3:10)
12. What would happen when the unclean spirits saw Him? (Mark 3:11)
13. What did Jesus earnestly warn the unclean spirits about? (Mark 3:12)

#9 GERASENES DEMONIAC (Matthew 8:28-32, Mark 5:1-13, Luke 8:26-23)

Once again we see the demonic influence on the physical being. We also see the unclean spirit go into unclean animals (pigs). I find I interesting that the man was vexed by the d-evil and when the swine encountered the swine (a whole herd) they (all) were vexed and all ran over a cliff into the see. The man became in his right mind.

DEMON-POSSESSED: daimonizomai (dahee-mon-id'-zom-ahee) = to be exercised by a daemon: - have a (be vexed with, be possessed with) devil (-s).

1. What was the condition of the two men who met Jesus when He arrived? (Matthew 8:28)
2. Where did these two men come out of? (Matthew 8:28)
3. What was the emotional condition of these men? (Matthew 8:28)
4. What were these demon possessed individuals preventing? (Matthew 8:28)
5. What did they cry out to Jesus? (Matthew 8:29)
6. What was at a distance from them, feeding? (Matthew 8:30)
7. What did the demons (that were in the men) begin to entreat Jesus about? (Matthew 8:31)
8. What one word did Jesus us to tell them what to do? (Matthew 8:32)
9. What was the cause and effect of the demons entering the swine? (Matthew 8:32)
10. What did the herdsmen (of the swine) do? (Matthew 8:33)
11. What was the cause and effect of the swine herdsmen's report? (Matthew 8:34)
12. What did the people of the city forcefully request (implored) Jesus to do? (Matthew 8:34)

#10 JAIRUS' DAUGHTER (Matthew 9:18-19, 23-25, Mark 5:22-24, 35-43, (Luke 8:26-33, 8:41=42)

The d-evil is no respecter of age or gender in his attacks on the physical body of human beings. This little girl was 12 years old (the same amount of time that the woman with the issue of blood, had the issue of blood.

NOTE: The disciples of John the Dipper came to Jesus asking Him about why fasting. John's disciples and the Pharisees fasted but Jesus' disciples did not fast. (See Matthew 9:15-17 for Jesus' response)

1. While Jesus was answering the disciples of John the Dipper who came to see Jesus? (Matthew 9:18)

NOTE: The leader in the synagogue was named Jairus. Jairus was a leader at the synagogue that Jesus attended in Capernaum, so he was familiar with the local guy who was healing people so when his little girl was at the point of death, he wanted Jesus to come and heal her. (Mark 5:22-23)

2. What posture did the synagogue leader take in front of Jesus? (Matthew 9:18)

3. What had happened to his daughter and what did he want Jesus to do? (Matthew 9:18)

4. What did Jesus do when He heard his request? (Matthew 9:19)

NOTE: Jesus encountered a woman who had an issue of blood for 12 years who stopped Him from going to see the leader's daughter. We will look at her story with our next (#11) questions.

5. After Jesus' encounter he continued to Jairus' house. When He entered the house, what did he see and hear? (Matthew 9:23)

6. What condition was the crowd in? (Matthew 9:23)

7. What did Jesus tell the noisy crowd? (Matthew 9:24)

NOTE: Death is called sleeping.

8. What did the crowd begin to do when He told them she was only sleeping and that she had not died? (Matthew 9:24)

NOTE: I believe that Jesus sent the noisy crowd out because they were not believers. Their negative doubts needed to leave so He could do his thing. Doubt hinders faith.

"And He did not do many miracles there because of their unbelief?"

Matthew 13:58

9. What did Jesus do when the crowd left? (Matthew 9:25)
10. What was the cause and effect when Jesus took the girl's hand? (Matthew 9:25)

#11 WOMAN WITH THE ISSUE OF BLOOD (Matthew 9:20-22, Mark 5:23-34, Luke 8:43-48)

Jesus was on His way to heal Jairus' (leader in the synagogue in Capernaum) 12 year old daughter. The daughter died (see previous questions). I find it interesting that the woman had an issue of blood for 12 years and Jairus' daughter was 12 years old. This woman who had a sickness (issue of blood, hemorrhage) for 12 years would come to be known as the healed woman.

1. With what was the woman suffering from? (Matthew 9:20)
2. How long had the woman had a hemorrhage (an issue of blood? (Matthew 9:20)
3. What is the medical history of the woman? (Mark 5:25-26)

NOTE: Many can relate to her medical history.
- She had a long term illness
- She saw many physicians
- She had spent all that she had
- She was not helped at all
- She had grown worse

4. Who did she hear about? (Mark 5:27)

5. When she heard about Jesus what did she keep saying to herself? (Matthew 9:21 The Amplified Bible)

"For she kept saying to herself, if I only touch His garment, I shall be restored to health."

Matthew 9:21, AMP

6. What was she saying to herself? (Matthew 9:21)

NOTE: She was speaking to herself, much like David did when he commanded his soul (mind, will, emotions) to "bless the Lord oh my soul" and as we saw in Matthew 9:21, AMP, she kept speaking to herself her desired results and no her 12 year experience.

7. After the woman heard about Jesus, and kept saying to herself desired results what corresponding action did the woman do with her faith? (Matthew 9:20, Mark 5:28, Luke 8:44)

8. What happened (Matthew 9:22, Mark 5:29, Luke 8:44)

9. When the woman touched Jesus's hem of His garment, what was Jesus' reaction? (Matthew 9:22, Mark 5:30, Luke 8:45-46)

NOTE: For 12 long years the woman went to many physicians, paid out all her money, and only got worse. She heard about Jesus (as he was going about and healing all who were harassed and oppressed by the d-evil, and she began to talk to herself and speaking desired result instead of what she had experienced for 12 years. She was using the Abraham method of speaking by calling things that are not as though they were instead of calling things that are as if they will never change. (Romans 4:17) She was doing what David did when he spoke to his soul. (Psalm 103:1) She was doing what David when he encouraged himself. (I Samuel 3:60) Then she got up, sought out Jesus, pressed through the crowd, got down way low and reached through the crowd and did exactly what she told herself she would do. The cause and effect was that Jesus felt the healing virtue flow out of him and she was instantly healed of a 12 year old disease.

NOTE TO THE NOTE: Many times when we are faced with a sickness we roll over like a dog and accept and identify with the sickness as the will of God on earth as it is in heaven. The only problem is that there is no sickness in heaven, no issues of blood, no cancer, no strokes, no diabetes, etc. What are you doing with the d-evil's attack on you? What are you

1. thinking
2. continually saying
3. doing?

#12 A FEW SICK PEOPLE (Matthew 13:53-58, Mark 6:55-56)

Jesus had just finished another one of His Parable Sessions. He departed and went to His hometown. I like this passage because it shows the importance of faith and healing/miracles. It shows that unbelief can negate faith for healing. I believe that is why Jesus went about and (1) taught (2) declared the

Kingdom will of God (3) Healed the sick. Many have asked me that since I believed in healing (and obviously they did not) why don't I go into the hospitals and heal them all. I don't believe that Jesus could heal everyone in the hospitals because of the people's unbelief; having more faith in the Physician's diagnosis and prognosis than in God's Word (His will).

1. Where did Jesus come to? (Matthew 13:54)
2. What was He doing in His hometown? (Matthew 13:54)
3. What was the reaction from the hometown crowd? (Matthew 13:54)
4. What questions did they ask? (Matthew 13:54-56)
5. What did they take? (Matthew 13:57)
6. What was Jesus' response to their offense? (Matthew 13:57)
7. What was Jesus not able to do? (Matthew 13:58)
8. Why could Jesus not do many miracles in His hometown? (Matthew 14:58)

NOTE: Some people ask me why if I believe in healing, why don't you go to the hospitals and empty them out by healing the sick? I don't believe that Jesus could do what they were asking because they were asking in unbelief.

#13 MULTITUDES # 3 (Matthew 14:34-36, Mark 6:55-56)

NOTE: Once again, we see Jesus ministering to the multitudes. He did this often. In our list of 41 incidences of healings 10 of those times were with multitudes and/or great multitudes.

NOTE: Jesus had just walked on the water, calmed the storm, and He came to the land of Gennesaret,

1. What did the men of that place do? (Matthew 14:35)
2. What did these men do when they recognized Him? (Matthew 14:35)

3. Where did they send the word into? (Matthew 14:34)
4. What happened when they ran about that whole country spreading the news? (Mark 6:55)
5. What did they carry the sick on? (Mark 6:55)
6. What happened wherever He entered villages or cities or countryside? (Mark 6:56)
7. What did they implore Him to do in the marketplace? (Mark 6:56)
8. What happened to those who touched the fringe of His cloak? (Mark 6:56, Matthew 14:36)

#14 THE SYROPHONICIAN'S DAUGHTER (Matthew 15:22-28, Mark 7:24)

I love the recount of this woman who had a daughter that was cruelly (the nature of the master of the demons, the d-evil) demon-possessed. She was not a covenant woman but a Canaanite woman and she knew that she did not have the right to make a request of Jesus. Jesus even acknowledge that she was not part of the sheepfold but was a dog.

1. What did the woman from the Canaanite region cry out to Jesus for? (Matthew 15:22)

MERCY: eleeō (el-eh-eh'-o) =From G1656; to compassionate (by word or deed, specifically by divine grace): - have compassion (pity on), have (obtain, receive, shew) mercy (on). G1656: eleos (el'-eh-os) =Of uncertain affinity; compassion (human or divine, especially active): - (+ tender) mercy.

2. What was here daughter's problem? (Matthew 15:22)
3. Did Jesus respond to her cry for mercy for her daughter? (Matthew 15:23)

4. What was the compassionate response from his disciples? (Matthew 15:23)

NOTE: Most likely they were following the lead of their Master.

5. When Jesus finally answered what was His response? (Matthew 15:24)

6. Did that stop the woman for begging for help? (Matthew 15:25)

NOTE: Israel was considered to be "the lost sheep of the house of Israel." (Matthew 15:24) At this time He was only sent to them. The Canaanite woman (a non-Covenant woman) was considered to be a dog.

7. When she bowed down before Jesus, what did she request? (Matthew 15:25)

NOTE: I think of Larry Gatlin's song *Help Me*, as he talks about being "on bended knees: as he was asking (begging) "please help me."

8. What did Jesus tell her that it was not good to do? (Matthew 15:27)

NOTE: If Jesus fed her the children's bread, it would be considered dog food (scraps).

9. What faith statement did the non-Covenant woman make? (Matthew 15:26)

"...Yes, lord; but even the dogs feed on the crumbs which fall from their masters table."

Matthew 15:27

10. What changed Jesus' mind? (Matthew 15:28)

11. What was the cause and effect on the daughter's condition? (Matthew 15:28)

#15. DEAF AND DUMB MAN (Mark 7:32-35)

People were always bringing people to Jesus to be healed. This time they brought Him someone who was "deaf and dumb." The word dumb does not mean mentally deficient but means unable to speak either with no speech or difficulty in speech.

1. What was the difficulty with the one they brought to Jesus? (Mark 7:32)
2. What did they implore Jesus to do? (Mark 7:32)

IMPLORE/BESEECH/CALL: parakaleō (par-ak-al-eh'-o) = to call near, that is, invite, invoke (by imploration, hortation or consolation): - beseech, call for, (be of good) comfort, desire, (give) exhort (-ation), intreat, pray.

NOTE: This was not just a polite request, it was a request full of compassion for this man.

3. What did Jesus first do with the man? (Mark 7:33)

NOTE: Many times Jesus did His healing in front of everyone, but at times He would take them to the side or ask people leave. Why? I don't know, but if I was to guess, I would think to remove them from doubters.

4. Jesus did a two-fold healing since he had two issues, deaf and could not speak. What did Jesus do first? (Mark 7:33)
5. How did Jesus deal with the man's deafness? (Mark 7:33)
6. How did He deal with the man's speech impediment? (Mark 7:33)

NOTE: Wow, fingers in the ear (deafness) and saliva on the tongue (speech impediment). I like to close my eyes and visualize what I am reading. Imagine if you will Jesus' fingers in the man's ears and then imagine Jesus "spitting" and then taking what he spit (saliva) and touching the man's tongue with the spittle. Imagine the Holy D.N.A.

NOTE: Notice that at this point with the finger-sticking and the spit, that the man was not yet healed. Let's see what happened next.

7.   Where did Jesus look up to? (Mark 7:34)

NOTE: I am convinced that Jesus was looking up to heaven where the answer (healing) would be coming from. I am reminded of one of the foundational verses for this book, Matthew 6:10, "Thy Kingdom (rule, reign, foundation of power) come (from headquarters), Thy Kingdom will be done (accomplished and manifested) on earth (where this deaf and speechless man was) as it is in heaven (headquarters, where there is no deafness and speech impediments)."

8.   When Jesus looked up to heaven what did Jesus breath out with? (Mark 7:34)

9.   What word did Jesus breathe out with a deep sigh? (Mark 7:34)

10. What did the word "Ephphatha!" mean? (Mark 7:34)

NOTE: Notice that Jesus did not beg God to open the ears or loosen the tongue. He spoke the desired results for the man, "be opened."

11. What was the cause and effect of Jesus doing these things? Name three things that happened. (Mark 7:35)

NOTE: The Kingdom will of God on earth as it is in heaven was (1) ears were opened (2) the impediment of his tongue was removed (3) he began speaking plainly.

12. What was Jesus' orders and did they obey? (Mark 7:36)

13. What was the crowd's response? (Mark 7:37)

#16 BLIND MAN (Mark 8:22-26)

In Acts 10:38 we see that Jesus went about (for three years) doing good, healing the sick that was brought on by the harassing and oppressing d-evil as Jesus manifested His purpose to destroy the works of the d-evil. (I John 3:18) Jesus had a custom in the synagogue where He would stand up and read. Someone handed Him the book of the prophet Isaiah and he opened it up to a specific place that He found and began to read from what we call (once the Bible was assigned chapters and verses) Isaiah 61:1-2. He read, "The Spirit of the Lord is upon Me because He anointed Me to:
1. Preach the Gospel to the poor
2. He has sent Me to proclaim release to the captives
3. He has sent me to proclaim recovery of sight to the blind
4. He has sent me to set free those who are oppressed
5. He has sent me to proclaim the favorable year of the Lord
We will now look at Jesus giving sight to the blind.
1. Where did they go after the feeding of the four thousand and his teaching for them to beware of the leaven of the Pharisees? (Mark 8:22)
2. Who did they bring to Jesus? (Mark 8:22)
3. What did they implore Jesus to do? (Mark 8:22)
4. What did Jesus take? (Mark 8:23)
5. Where did Jesus take/lead the blind man? (Mark 8:23)
6. What two things did Jesus do to the blind man? (Mark 8:23)
7. After Jesus spit in the blind man's and then laid His hands on Him, what did Jesus ask the blind man? (Mark 8:23)
8. What was the blind man's response after he looked up? (Mark 8:24)

NOTE: Sometimes we expect immediate results when someone prays for us, especially if it is Jesus doing the praying.

9. What did Jesus do? (Mark 8:25)
10. How hard did the blind man look the second time? (Mark 8:25)
11. When the blind man looked intently the second time, what did he begin to do? (Mark 8:25)
12. Once he was healed and could see clearly, what instructions did Jesus give him when he was sent home? (Mark 8:26)

NOTE: I love this account of healing. There was not an immediate response but there was a partial healing. Things were blurry. Jesus did not throw His hands up and declare that it must not be the will of God to heal the blind man. No, Jesus touched Him a second time. This is where we get the phrase, God is the God of the second touch. Never give up. Jesus laid His hands on him a second time. The cause and effect was restoration of sight. I also like the fact that Jesus had to lead him out of the village because he was blind, but after he was healed, Jesus sent him on by himself without any help, because he could now see. Jesus' anointing was working.

 # 17 CHILD WITH AN EVIL SPIRIT (Matthew 17:14-18, Mark 9:14-17, Luke 9:38-43)

The d-evil is an equal opportunity cause of sickness and disease. Again, we see that there is a connection of demonic activity and sickness and when Jesus dealt with the cause the boy was cured at once.

1. Jesus is on the move again. What/Who did they come to? (Matthew 17:14)

2. Who came to Jesus as He came to the crowd? (Matthew 17:14)

NOTE: When was the last time you came to Jesus with a healing need?

3. What position the man assume when he came to Jesus? (Matthew 17:14)
4. What did the man ask Jesus for? (Matthew 17:15)
5. Who was the requested mercy for? (Matthew 17:15)
6. What were the four symptoms of the song? (Matthew 17:15)
7. Who did he bring his son to first? (Matthew 17:16)
8. What were the results of bringing the son to the disciples? (Matthew 17:16)

JESUS' RESPONSE:

"And Jesus answered and said, you unbelieving and perverted generation, ho long shall I be with you? How long shall I put up with you...?"

Matthew 17:17

9. After Jesus expressed His view on their inability to handle the situation, what did Jesus request? (Matthew 17:17)
10. What did Jesus do? (Matthew 17:18)
11. What was the cause and effect (2 things) that happened when Jesus rebuked him? (Matthew 17:18)

CURE: therapeuō (ther-ap-yoo'-o)= to wait upon menially, that is, (figuratively) to adore (God), or (specifically) to relieve (of disease): - cure, heal, worship.

12. How quickly was the son cured? (Matthew 17:18)

NOTE: The blind man was healed but needed a second touch for the manifestation of sight, while the boy was healed immediately.

13. How did the disciples come to Jesus after he boy was cured? (Matthew 17:19)
14. What question did the disciples have? (Matthew 17:19)
15. What was Jesus answer to their question? (Matthew 17:19)
16. What was the minimum amount of faith needed to cure the boy? (Matthew 17:20)

NOTE: Their faith must have been smaller than the size of a mustard seed. When I study faith I see that there are stages of healing. Faith smaller than a mustard seed, mustard seed size, large faith, great faith, and ever increasing faith. I believe that our faith is grown by exercising it and feeding it with the Word of God. I also believe that we can face starvation of faith and have what is known in the medical field, as failure to thrive. Failure to thrive is where a patient has access to all the food and drink they need but they don't eat or drink with the cause and effect being dehydration and malnourishment.

#18 BLIND BARTIMAEUS (Matthew 20:30-34, Mark 10:46-53, Luke 18:35-43)

Jesus continues on with healing the blind. In the Matthew account it speaks of two blind men being healed. In the Mark and Luke account it only mentions one blind man. Some say there were two men but Bart was the more aggressive, all I know is that someone was blind and someone was healed.

1. Where did this healing take place? (Mark 10:46)
2. Did this healing take place as they entered or when they were leaving? (Mark 10:46)

166

3. Did the healing take place in a large crowd or a small gathering? (Mark 10:46)
4. Who is the blind beggar identified as? (Mark 10:46)
5. Where was Blind Bart sitting? (Mark 10:46)
6. What did he cry out when he heard that it was Jesus the Nazarene? (Mark 10:47)
7. What did Bart desire from Jesus? (Mark 10:47)

NOTE: Being healed and getting mercy from God is the same thing. Mercy means you get what you don't deserve.

MERCY: eleeō (el-eh-eh'-o)=From G1656; to compassionate (by word or deed, specifically by divine grace): - have compassion (pity on), have (obtain, receive, shew) mercy (on). G1656: eleos (el'-eh-os)= Of uncertain affinity; compassion (human or divine, especially active): - (+ tender) mercy.

8. What was the response of many people? (Mark 10:48)
9. How did the people tell Bart to be quite? (Mark 10:48)
10. What did Bart do? (Mark 10:48)
11. What did Jesus do when He heart Bart's cry for mercy? (Mark 10:49)
12. What did the people do when Jesus told them to "call him here" (Mark 10:49)
13. What did Blind Bart do? (Mark 10:50)
14. What did Jesus ask him about what he wanted? (Mark 10:51)
15. What did Blind Bart want Rabboni (teacher) to do? (Mark 10:51)

NOTE: Again, Bartimaeus was crying out for mercy. Mercy in his mind was to not be blind, to be healed.

16. What did Jesus tell Blind Bart to do? (Mark 10:52)
17. What did Jesus see in Bartimaeus. (Mark 10:52)

18. How was Blind Bart's faith manifested? (Mark 10:52)
19. What did Jesus tell him to do? (Mark 10:52)
20. What happened immediately as He told him to go? (Mark 10:52)
21. What did Blind Bartimaeus do when he regained his sight? (Mark 10:52)

19 CENTURION'S SERVANT (Matthew 8:5-13, Luke 7:2-10)

Jesus' healings were not limited to the "Chosen People," the Jewish nation. More than once a Gentile (non-Jewish, non-covenant) experienced healing. It was not limited to common people but also people in authority.

1. What city did Jesus enter? ("Jesus made Capernaum his home during the years of his ministry: Leaving Nazareth he went and lived in Capernaum." (Matt 4:13)." (Bible Places.com)
2. Who came to Jesus? (Matthew 4:13)
3. What was this man's occupation? (Matthew 4:5)

CENTURION: hekatontarchēs hekatontarchos (hek-at-on-tar'-khace, hek-at-on-tar'-khos): the captain of one hundred men: - centurion.

4. What did the centurion do? (Matthew 8:5)
5. What was the condition of his servant? (Matthew 8:6)
6. What was the emotions of the servant in his torment? (Matthew 8:6)
7. What did Jesus say that He would do? (Matthew 8:7)
8. What was the centurion's response when Jesus said He would come? (Matthew 8:7)

9. What was the centurion's suggestion to Jesus instead of coming to his home? (Matthew 8:7)

NOTE: We see the power of words, especially Jesus'Words. We also see that there is no distance in healing. Jesus could be smack dab in the middle of a multitude or just speak the Word.

10. What would be the cause and effect of Jesus speaking "the word?" (Matthew 8:8)

11. What did the centurion understand and why? (Matthew 8:9)

AUTHORITY/POWER: exousia (ex-oo-see'-ah)= (in the sense of ability); privilege, that is, (subjectively) force, capacity, competency, freedom, or (objectively) mastery (concretely magistrate, superhuman, potentate, token of control), delegated influence: - authority, jurisdiction, liberty, power, right, strength. (See Matthew 28:18)

POWER: dunamis (doo'-nam-is)=From G1410; force (literally or figuratively); specifically miraculous power (usually by implication a miracle itself): - ability, abundance, meaning, might (-ily, -y, -y deed), (worker of) miracle (-s), power, strength, violence, mighty (wonderful) work. G 1410: dunamai (doo'-nam-ahee)=Of uncertain affinity; to be able or possible: - be able, can (do, + -not), could, may, might, be possible, be of power. (See Acts 10:38)

NOTE: Jesus had authority/power (exousia) , the right to do what He did as it was delegated from the Father. Jesus also had power/dynamic ability (dunamis) to do what He was authorized to do. The believer (those who trust in, clings to, relies on and adheres to) who believes in the Word of God has that same authority that Jesus had. It is like the authority coming from Washington down to the local principalities. The police have the right to enforce the laws of the land (not misuse) and they also have the power (fire power) to do what is need to enforce those laws.

12. What was Jesus' response when he heard the centurion's explanation of authority? (Matthew 8:10)

13. What had Jesus not found with anyone in Israel? (Matthew 8:10)

NOTE: We see once again that this thing called faith can be smaller than the size of a mustard seed, as small as a mustard seed, weak, small, large, and ever increasing. Faith comes by hearing the Word of God concerning Christ and the Words that Christ taught.

14. What did Jesus say about non-Jewish believers (Gentiles) and their relation to the Kingdom of heaven? (Matthew 8:11)

15. What did Jesus say about the "sons of the Kingdom (Jewish chosen people) who did not have faith? (Matthew 8:12)

16. What did Jesus tell the centurion? (Matthew 8:13)

17. What was the cause and effect? (Matthew 8:13)

20 TWO BLIND MEN (Matthew 9:27-30)

Once again Jesus is healing the blind.

1. What were these two blind men doing? (Matthew 9:27)

2. What were they crying out? (Matthew 9:27)

NOTE: Shades of Blind Bartimaeus.

3. What did the call Jesus? (Matthew 9:27)

4. Was Jesus out in the open all the time? If not, where was he? (Matthew 9:27)

5. What did the Jesus do/ask when the blind men came up to Him? (Matthew 9:28)
6. What was the response to Jesus' question? (Matthew 9:28)

"…do you believe (trust in, cling to, rely on, adhere to) that I am able to do this…?"

Matthew 9:28

"…they said to Him, Yes, Lord."

Matthew 9:28

7. Once Jesus established what they could or could not believe concerning their healing, what did He do? (Matthew 9:28)
8. What did He say to them as He touched their eyes? (Matthew 9:28)

NOTE: If Jesus was a healer (and He was) and He could heal (and He did) why did Jesus not go to all of the hospitals and empty the out by healing all the sick? Yes, my tongue is in my check as I type this, but I have been asked this about myself—since I believed in healing why don't I go through the hospital and empty them out. Jesus went to His own hometown and he could do no major miracles but only heal a few minor ailments. Why? Because of unbelief. That is why He asked these blind men if they believed.

"And he did not many mighty works there because of their unbelief."

Matthew 13:58
KJV

171

9. What was the cause and effect of Jesus touching their eyes and speaking? (Matthew 9:30)
10. What did Jesus sternly say to them? (Matthew 9:30)
11. What did they do? (Matthew 9:31)

21 DUMB DEMONIAC (Matthew 9:32-34)

The word "dumb" does not speak of his cognitive abilities, but of his inability to speak. As a Speech-Language Pathologist, I love to see Jesus doing speech therapy.

DUMB: kōphos (ko-fos') = blunted, that is, (figuratively) of hearing (deaf) or speech (dumb): - deaf, dumb, speechless.

1. Who was brought to Jesus? (Matthew 9:32-33)
2. What happened when Jesus cast out the demon? (Matthew 9:33)

NOTE: I want to make sure you understand that not every person who has a speech impediment is demon possessed, however if you have been studying these passages of Jesus healing, he did not ignore or focus on demons, but He did go to the root of some of the healings.

> *"He sent His word (Jesus and His thoughts about what He wanted to happen) and healed them and delivered them from their destructions."*
>
> Psalm 107:19

3. What were the crowds? (Matthew 9:33)
4. What has not ever been seen in Israel? (Matthew 9:33)
5. What were the Pharisees saying? (Matthew 9:34)

6. How did the Pharisees say that Jesus cast out the demons? (Matthew 9:34)

NOTE: There is a thing called "blasphemy of the Holy Spirit," also known as the "unpardonable sin." It is the one thing that cannot be forgiven. (Mark 3:28-29, Matthew 12:31-32, Luke 12:10) This thing called "blasphemy of the Holy Spirt" has been identified as "adultery," "divorce," (fill in the blank of any sin that will not be forgiven). Jesus identifies what "the blasphemy of the Holy Ghost" is.

> *"And everyone who speaks a word against the Son of Man (Jesus) it will be forgiven him; BUT he who blasphemes against the Holy Spirit, it will not be forgiven him."*
>
> Luke 12:10
> with addition and emphasis mine

Mark not only identifies what the "blasphemy of the Holy Spirit" is but also defines that that means.

> *"Truly I say to you, all sins shall be forgiven the sons of men, and whatever blasphemies the other (so it is words that you speak, not what you physically do); but whoever blasphemes against the Holy Spirit never has forgiveness, but is guilty of an eternal sin, because they (Pharisees/religious leaders) were saying, He (Jesus) has an unclean spirit."*
>
> Mark 3:28-30
> with addition mine

Matthew puts it this way,

> *"...whoever speaks against the Holy Spirit, it shall not*

173

be forgiven him, either in this age or in the age to come."
Matthew 12:32

It seems to me that Jesus was accused of casting out demons by the power of demons, thus attributing the works of the Spirit to the works of demons.

22 BLIND AND DUMB DEMONIAC (Matthew 12:22-31, Luke 11:14)

Once again, Jesus is healing and casting out demons. Once again, religious people attribute to satan the works of the Holy Spirit. This happened back in the "Bible days," but these are also considered the "Bible days" and people are still attributing to Christians who believe in healing and practice laying on of hands, as demonic.

1. What was the man possessed with? (Matthew 12:22)
2. What two things were the cause and effect of the demon possessed man? (Matthew 12:22)
3. What did Jesus do? (Matthew 12:22)
4. What was the cause and effect of Jesus healing the man? (Matthew 12:22)
5. What was the reaction of the crowd? (Mathew 12:23)

NOTE: The people were looking for the Messiah and they were questioning whether or not Jesus (from Nazareth) could be the Messiah (their deliverer). Of course we can see easily that yes He can!

6. While the crowds were amazed, what was the response from the Pharisees (the religious leaders of the crowd)? (Matthew 12:24)

NOTE: The Pharisees (who were not fair), attributed the healing power of Jesus to demons and the head demon Beelzebul.

7. What did Jesus know? (Matthew 12:25)
8. What did Jesus reveal to them about His known thoughts and about their thoughts? (Matthew 12:25)

NOTE: Jesus turns their twisted logic and straightens it out.

9. What is satan if he casts out satan? (Matthew 12:26)
10. If satan is against satan, what is the status of satan's kingdom? (Matthew 12:26)

NOTE: Jesus then turns the example to their sons who cast out demons. "If by Beelzebul (ruler of the demons) by whom do your sons cast them out?" (Matthew 12:27) It was for this reason they (the Pharisees) will be judged.

11. What would be the result *if* (and He did) cast out demons by the Spirit of God, what had come upon them? (Matthew 12:28)

NOTE: Jesus gave another example about the strong man's house. He asks them,

"How can anyone enter the strong man's house and carry of his property, unless he fist binds the strong man? And then he will plunder his house."

Matthew 12:30

The strong man (demons) was bound by the Strong Man (Jesus) who bound the demon and plundered the house (the man who was possessed. (Matthew 12:29)

12. What was the ones (the Pharisees) who were not with Jesus in this? (Matthew 12:30)
13. What is someone who does not gather do? (Matthew 12:30)
14. What shall be forgiven? (Matthew 12:31)
15. What will not be forgiven? (Matthew 12:31)

NOTE: As seen previously we see that this thing called "blasphemy of the Holy Spirit" is like the Pharisees were doing, attributing the work of the Holy Spirit to demons.

23 MULTITUDES #4 (Matthew 4:23-25, Luke 6:17-19)

Once again we see Jesus moving through the multitudes and healing people. There are 10 times that we will see Jesus healing in the multitudes. Yes, He healed individual people and we see that individual people also made up the multitudes.

1. Where was Jesus going? (Matthew 4:23)
2. What did Jesus do in their synagogues as He went about in all Galilee? (Matthew 4:23)
3. What did Jesus proclaim and declare as He went about in all Galilee? (Matthew 4:23)
4. What did Jesus demonstrate as He taught and declared? (Matthew 4:23)
5. Who did they bring to Him out of the multitudes? (Matthew 4:23)

NOTE: They brought to Jesus: (Matthew 4:24)
- The ill
- Suffering with various diseases
- People with pains
- Demoniacs
- Epileptics
- Paralytics

6. What did Jesus do to them all? (Matthew 4:24)
7. Who followed Him from Galilee, the Decapolis, Jerusalem, Judea and beyond the Jordan? (Matthew 4:25)
8. After Jesus went off to a mountain to pray, what did He do? (Luke 6:17)

9. Where did He stand? (Luke 6:17)

10. Who was in the large (multitude) crowd? (Luke 6:17)

11. Who else was there? (Luke 6:17)

NOTE: There was a large crowd and a great throng, aka a multitude of people.

12. Why did all of these people come to see Jesus? (Luke 6:18)

NOTE: People needed to be (a) healed of their diseases (b) troubled with unclean spirits. (c) needing to cured

13. What were all the people trying to do? (Luke 6:19)

14. What was coming from Jesus? (Luke 6:19)

POWER: dunamis (doo'-nam-is)=From G1410; force (literally or figuratively); specifically miraculous power (usually by implication a miracle itself): - ability, abundance, meaning, might (-ily, -y, -y deed), (worker of) miracle (-s), power, strength, violence, mighty (wonderful) work G1410: dunamai (doo'-nam-ahee)=Of uncertain affinity; to be able or possible: - be able, can (do, + -not), could, may, might, be possible, be of power.

POWER: exerchomai (ex-er'-khom-ahee)= to issue (literally or figuratively): - come-(forth, out), depart (out of), escape, get out, go (abroad, away, forth, out, thence), proceed (forth), spread abroad

15. What was the cause and effect of the power that was coming from Him? (Luke 6:19)

NOTE: This was the same virtue that flowed out of Jesus when the woman with the issue of blood, reached out and touched the hem of His garment. This does not say that Jesus was touching everybody, but that they were touching Him (by faith) and the healing flowed with the cause and effect that they were healed.

HEALING: iaomai (ee-ah'-om-ahee)= a primary verb; to cure (literally or figuratively): - heal, make whole.

24 MULTITUDES #5 (Matthew 9:35-36)

1. Where was Jesus going through? (Matthew 9:35)
2. As Jesus went through all the cities and villages, what was He doing in their synagogues? (Matthew 9:35)
3. What was Jesus proclaiming/declaring? (Matthew 9:35)
4. What was Jesus healing? (Matthew 9:35)
5. When Jesus saw the people, what did He feel for them? (Matthew 9:36)
6. Why did He feel this way about them? (Matthew 9:36)
7. What did Jesus say to His disciples? (Matthew 9:37-38)

NOTE: Jesus was surrounded by many people who were sick with every kind of dis-ease and sickness, and they were distressed and dispirited. The harvest was plentiful (many people needed healing, but Jesus was only one man, and there needed to be workers sent out to do the same thing that Jesus was doing. Jesus told His disciples before He went to the cross that if they believed the works that He did, they would being doing greater works because He was going back to the Father, and He was going to send the Holy Spirit back to them. Jesus then said that if they asked Him anything in His name that He will do it (the works of healing). Jesus was going to die on the cross, be buried, and then be raised from the dead on the third day. This was the work that only He could do, but the works that they would be doing would be as witnesses (a noun) as they witnessed (a verb) about Jesus but also healing and delivering those who were distressed and dispirited. (Matthew 9:35, John 14:11-14)

25 MULTITUDE # 6 (Matthew 11:4-5, Luke 7:21)

Jesus had given instructions to His 12 disciples, He departed from there to teach and preach in their cities (where there would be large crowds as usual). John the Baptist (the dipper into water not the denomination) had heard of the works of Christ (the Anointed One, the Messiah) while he was in prison. He sent word by his disciples to ask Jesus if He was the expected one (the Christ) or if they should look for someone else? (Matthew 11:1-3) Jesus' response was linked to the works.

1. What did Jesus tell John's disciples to go back and tell him? (Matthew 11:4)

NOTE: John's disciples had heard and seen Jesus in action, so Jesus told them to go back to the prison that John was in and report what they (1) saw (visual miracles and healings) and heard (what others were saying or demons leaving the bodies).

2. What were the blind receiving? (Matthew 11:5)
3. What were the lame doing? (Matthew 11:5)
4. What was happening to the lepers? (Matthew 11:5)
5. What were the deaf doing? (Matthew 11:5)
6. What was happening to the dead? (Matthew 11:5)
7. What was being done for the poor? (Matthew 11:5)
8. When John's disciples went back to him with their report, what was Jesus doing at that very time? (Luke 7:17)

NOTE: Jesus was curing many people. Jesus cured (Luke 7:21-22)

- Diseases
- Afflictions
- Evil spirits
- Giving sight to blind
- The lamed walked
- Lepers cleansed
- Deaf hear
- Dead are raised up

NOTE: Jesus said, "Blessed is he who does not take offense at Me." I know it is hard to imagine but there were people who were taking offense at Jesus healing and there are many people now who take offense at Jesus healing (through His people) now.

26 MULTITUDES # 7 (Matthew14:14, Luke 9:11, John 6:2)

Once again Jesus was face with a large crowd. When Jesus heard (it was reported to Him) about John being murdered/executed/beheaded, He withdrew in a boat to a secluded place by Himself. Once again He felt compassion for them, and once again He healed the sick out of compassion.

1. What did Jesus feel for the large crowd? (Matthew 14:4)
2. What did Jesus to the people who followed Him as He was seeking conclusion? (Luke 9:11)
3. What did Jesus speak to them about? (Luke 9:11)
4. After speaking to them about the Kingdom of God, what did Jesus to those who needed a healing? (Luke (9:11)
5. What did the large crowd that followed Him see? (John 6:2)
6. What was Jesus performing? (John 6:2)
7. Who were these signs performed upon? (John 6:2)

SIGNS/MIRACLES: sēmeion (say-mi'-on) =; an indication, especially ceremonially or supernaturally: - miracle, sign, token, wonder.

SICK/DIS-EASE: astheneō (as-then-eh'-o) =From G772; to be feeble (in any sense): - be diseased, impotent folk (man), (be) sick, (be, be made) weak. G772: asthenēs (as-then-ace') =strengthless (in various applications, literally, or figuratively and morally): - more feeble, impotent, sick, without strength, weak (-er, -ness, thing).

#27 GREAT MULTITUDES #8 (Matthew 15:30-31)

Jesus is sitting on a mountain when a large crowed (not just a crowd but a large crowd, aka a multitude). The large crowed did not just come by themselves, they brought some-one with them.

1. Who did the large crowd bring with them? (Matthew 15:30)
2. Besides the large crowd bringing the lame, crippled, blind and mute, how many others did they bring? (Matthew 15:30)
3. Where did they lay down the lame, crippled, blind and mute and many others? (Matthew 15:30)
4. What did Jesus do to the lame, crippled, blind and mute and many others? (Matthew 15:30)

HEALED: therapeuō (ther-ap-yoo'-o) = to wait upon meni-ally, that is, (figuratively) to adore (God), or (specifically) to relieve (of disease): - cure, heal, worship.

5. What was the crowd's response to seeing Jesus heal the

lame, crippled, blind, mute and many others? (Matthew 15:31)

NOTE: Here is a list of what Jesus did with those who were lame, crippled, blind, mute,and many others. (Matthew 15:31)

- Mute were speaking
- Crippled were restored
- Lame were walking
- Blind were seeing

6. Who did the people they (the large crowd/large multitude) glorify?

NOTE: By now, as you have read through this book and been doing the workbook section you may see that I believe that all of this healing that Jesus is doing is, "Thy will be done on earth as it is in heaven." (Matthew 6:10) We see that as He healed He was fulfilling His purpose of "destroying the works of the d-evil." (I John 3:8) We see that Jesus was going about with the Anointing of the Holy Ghost and dynamic ability (power) doing good (and not bad) and healing all (everyone that you have studied about thus far) who were harassed and oppressed by the d-evil for God was with Him (Immanuel God with us). (Acts 10:38, Matthew 1:23)

#28 GREAT MULTITUDES # 9 (Matthew 19:2)

Jesus had finished another teaching session and then departed from Galilee as He went about doing good, teaching, proclaiming/declaring the Gospel/Good News and healing the sick. He enters the region of Judea beyond the Jordan.

1. Who followed Him? (Matthew 19:2)
2. What did He do to those who were there (in the region of Judea beyond the Jordan)? (Matthew 19:2)

NOTE: Remember Jesus' Modus Operandi (M.O.) Jesus for three years with the anointing of the Holy Ghost and power (duNAmis, dynamic ability) went about doing good (and not bad) but healing (to cure (literally or figuratively): - heal, make whole) all who were harassed and oppressed (dominated by the d-evil) by the d-evil (evil one, satan, stealer, killer, destroyer). (Acts 10:38)

NOTE: Remember that we only see a thumbnail sketch of the signs that Jesus performed. There were many things that "were not written in this book." (John 20:30) The things that were written in the book of John were written for the purpose that you might believe that Jesus is the Christ (the Anointed One anointed with the Holy Ghost and dynamic ability healing all who were harassed and oppressed by the d-evil and that by believing (trusting in, clinging to, relying on, adhering to) you may have life (not death) in His name. (John 20:31)

29 BLIND AND LAME IN THE TEMPLE (Matthew 21:14)

Jesus was on a mission and part of that mission was cleaning house. Jesus entered the temple and drove out all those who were buying and selling in the temple, and overturned the tables of the moneychangers and the seats of those who were selling doves. Many people apply this to people selling product in church, but I don't think this applies. People in the temple were charging many shekels to buy animals for sacrifices and the money changers were changing money to proper coinage. Jesus quotes from Isaiah and Jeremiah, "My house shall be called a house of prayer; but you are making it a robbers' den." I like that Jesus who was God in the flesh (John 1:1-14) took ownership of His house.

1. Who came to Jesus in the temple? (Matthew 21:14)

NOTE: My Ryrie Study Bible notes points out that most likely the blind and the lame came to him at the gate of temple or the temple court because the blind and lame were not permitted into the temple. (II Samuel 5:8)

2. What did Jesus to those who came to Him? (Matthew 21:14)

3. Who saw the wonderful things Jesus had done? (Matthew 21:15)

WONDERFUL: thaumasios (thow-mas'-ee-os) = wondrous, that is, (neuter as noun) a miracle: - wonderful thing.

NOTE: When I see the word *wonderful* I like to say, *full of wonder.*

4. What were the children shouting? (Matthew 21:15)

NOTE: Hosanna means to *save now.* Saved from what or who? From the oppression of Rome and maybe the religious tyranny of scribes and chief priests.

5. What did the scribes and chief priests become? (Matthew 21:15)

INDIGNANT/SORE DISTRESSED aganakteō (ag-an-ak-teh'-o)=From agan (much) and grief; akin to the base of G43); to be greatly afflicted, that is, (figuratively) indignant: - be much (sore) displeased, have (be moved with, with) indignation.

6. What did Jesus say came out of the mouth infants and nursing babies according to Psalm 28:2, Matthew 21:16?

NOTE: Concerning healing the religious still are indignant

more over healing of human beings than being indignant over financial profiteering in the temple.

30 WIDOW'S SON (Luke 7:11-17)

Once again Jesus was on the move. He was not limited by a seat in the synagogue, or sitting on His good intentions on a pew. If they had a pew (a long bench with a back, placed in rows in the main part of some churches to seat the congregation) in the synagogue it would most likely be a rock which would be hard on the good intentions they were seated on. We complain with a nice padded pew. Of course some of us come with natural padding.

1. Who was going with Jesus to Nain (10 miles Southeast of Nazareth)? (Luke 7:11)
2. Who accompanied Jesus and His disciples? (Luke 7:11)
3. As they approached Nain what did they run into? (Luke 7:12)
4. Who was the dead man the only son of? (Luke 7:12)
5. Who was with the widow? (Luke 7:12)
6. What emotion did Jesus feel when Jesus saw her? (Luke 7:13)

COMPASSION: splagchnizomai (splangkh-nid'-zom-ahee) = to have the bowels yearn, that is, (figuratively) feel sympathy, to pity: - have (be moved with) compassion.

7. What did Jesus touched when He came up? (Luke 7:13)
8. What did Jesus tell the widow to not do? (Luke 7:13)

WEEP: klaiō (klah'-yo)= to sob, that is, wail aloud (whereas G1145 is rather to cry silently): - bewail, weep.

185

NOTE: I don't think Jesus is against weeping at the loss of a loved one. After all, Jesus wept (to shed tears). (John 11:35) Jesus saw Mary weeping (sobbing, wailing loudly) for her dead brother and Jesus' friend Lazuraus. Jesus saw her weeping (sobbing, wailing loudly) and the crowd with her also weeping (sobbing, wailing loudly). Jesus was deeply moved in His human spirit and He was troubled. Jesus' weeping (crying silently) is contrasted to weeping of others (sobbing and weeping loudly).

9. What did Jesus touch? (Luke 7:14)

COFFIN: soros (sor-os') = a funereal receptacle (urn, coffin), that is, (by analogy) a bier: - bier.

10. What did the coffin bearers do? (Luke 7:14)
11. What did Jesus speak to the widow's young man? (Luke 7:14)

ARISE: egeirō (eg-i'-ro)= to waken (transitively or intransitively), that is, rouse (literally from sleep, from sitting or lying, from disease, from death; or figuratively from obscurity, inactivity, ruins, nonexistence): - awake, lift (up), raise (again, up), rear up, (a-) rise (again, up), stand, take up.

12. What was the cause and effect of Jesus speaking to the dead man? (Luke 7:15)
13. When the dead man arose at Jesus' command to arise, what did he do after he rose? (Luke 7:15)
14. What did Jesus do with the risen man? (Luke 7:15)
15. What was the emotional reaction of the people? (Luke 7:16)
16. What did they begin to do? (Luke 7:16)

17. What did they say about the local boy from Nazareth? (Luke 7:16)
18. Who had visited them when Jesus visited them? (Luke 7:16, John 1:1-14)
19. What went out concerning Jesus? (Luke 7:17)

31 MARY MAGDALENE And Others (Luke 8:2)

The M.O. (Modus Operandi) continues. A woman (most likely Mary Magdalene, a prostitute caught in adultery, forgiven, delivered from seven demons had just broken an alabaster box full of precious perfume over Jesus' feet and her tears fell on His feet also and she dried his feet with her hair. Why was she weeping? She was forgiven. The religious lot condemned Him and her but not only did Jesus have the smell of worship on His feet, the smell of worship was all in the woman's hair. When we truly worship at the feet of Jesus, the smell of that worship should carry on wherever we go. If you go down in the water with someone to be baptized, when they come out of the water, and you hug them, you also get wet.

1. Where was Jesus going around? (Luke 8:1)
2. What was He doing in the cities and villages? (Luke 8:1)
3. Who was with Jesus? (Luke 8:2)
4. What had happened to some of the women who were with Him and the twelve? (Luke 8:2)
5. How many demons did Jesus cast of Mary Magdalene? (Luke 8:2)

NOTE: If you had seven demons cast out of you, wouldn't you fall at His feet and worship Him?

6. What was Joanna (the wife of Chusza, Herod's steward) and Susanna, and many others doing? (Luke 8:3)

NOTE: Sometimes we think of Jesus going around with no visible means of support, but in reality people gave their money to Him and supported Him out of their private means.

32 CRIPPLED WOMAN (Luke 13:10-17)

Once again the Teacher (Rabbi) was teaching in the synagogues. We first saw the Teacher (Rabbi) teaching about His anointing, that He went about doing good and healing all who were oppressed by the d-evil. (Acts 10:38) I believe that wherever He went for three years His teaching was about His anointing (from Isaiah 61:1-2), then He would declare God's Kingdom will on earth as it is in heaven, and then He healed the sick. This time we see Him teaching and then healing on the Sabbath, a no-no to any "good Jew." Oh by the way, did you know that Jesus was a Jew who had deep roots in the Old Testament? Many New Testament believers negate the Old Testament, but when they do they miss out on understanding what the New Testament is all about.

1. Where was Jesus teaching? (Luke 13:10)
2. How long had a woman been sick? (Luke 13:11)
3. What was her sickness caused by? (Luke 13:11)
4. What was the cause and effect of this sickness caused by a spirit? (Luke 13:11)
5. What could she *not* do? (Luke 13:11)

NOTE: As I see many sick people, they are faced with impossibilities of what they cannot do. That is hard on the faith when you try to walk by faith but you are walking by sight. Jesus saw beyond what He saw, and saw and heard what the Father did and said. We need to do that as we pray about seemingly impossible situations and circumstances spiritually, emotionally, physically, and financially.

6. What did Jesus do when He saw her? (Luke 13:11)

NOTE: Sometimes we do not have to wait for someone to ask us to pray for them. If we are walking in the Spirit and the gifts of the Spirit are flowing like a word of knowledge and a word of wisdom along with the gifts (plural of the Spirit) and the fruit of the Spirit are growing, we can call someone over.

7. What did Jesus say to the woman once she came over? (Luke 13:12)

NOTE: He declared the will of God for her in spite of her still being bent over.

8. What did Jesus do besides speaking forth desired results by calling things that are *not* as though they were instead of calling things that *are* as if they will *never* change? (Luke 13:13, Romans 4:17)

9. What was the cause and effect of Jesus speaking and laying on of hands? (Luke 13:13)

10. What did she begin to do after being bent over for 18 years? (Luke 13:13)

11. While the woman was glorifying the Lord, what synagogue official's response? (Luke 13:13)

12. Why was the synagogue official indignant? (Luke 13:14)

13. What was the synagogue official's excuse to the crowd for his indignation? (Luke 13:14)

14. What did Jesus call the synagogue official? (Luke 13:15)

HYPOCRITE: hupokritēs (hoop-ok-ree-tace'= From G5271; an actor under an assumed character (stage player), that is, (figuratively) a dissembler ("hypocrite"): - hypocrite.

G527: hupokrinomaHEE (hoop-ok-rin'-om-ahee)= To decide (speak or act) under a false part, that is, (figuratively) dissemble (pretend): - feign

NOTE: Back in 1970, I was born again, saved, became a Christ Follower. One of my friends told me when I called him up and gave him the good news, that I was a hypocrite. I was devastated until later on in Bible School, I saw that in the Greek language a hypocrite wore a mask like in a Greek play, playing someone they were not. I realized that I was not playing a part, but my friend was as he denied his need for a Savior. So it is with religious leaders back in Jesus' day feigning indignation over the will of God being manifested on the Sabbath Day.

15. What could they do on Sabbath Day? (Luke 13:15)

16. What did Jesus say this woman was? (Luke 13:16)

NOTE: "Being a descendant of Abraham, this female was possessed of his faith, and because of it, was in the Lord's house on the Lord's Day. As an inheritress of Abraham she was in the right place to be healed. Although a firm believer in Jehovah she yet was afflicted for a long time. However her painful malady did not keep her from attendance at the synagogue. Walking must have been difficult for her, but her seat was never vacant when the Sabbath came around. Think of what she would have missed if she had absented herself from God's house that Sabbath when Jesus visited it! What encouragement this faithful daughter of Abraham brings to all godly women, who, in spite of bodily infirmities, household cares and chores, find their way to the sanctuary where the Lord is ever present to undertake for true worshipers."(Bible Gateway commentary on being a daughter of Abraham)

NOTE TO THE NOTE: Reading Galatians 3:10-14

we see that Jesus hung on a tree (the old rugged Cross) and became a curse so we would not be cursed. Part of not being cursed is found in verse 4, "in order that in Christ Jesus the blessing of Abraham might come to the Gentiles (non-covenant people), so that we would receive the promise of the Spirit (Holy) through faith."

17. Who had bound the woman for 18 years of being bent over? (Luke 13:16)

NOTE: The will of God was not for her to be bent over for 18 years. That was the will of the d-evil/satan. The will of God on earth as it is in heaven was to be healed.

18. Who was humiliated? (Luke 13:16)
19. Who was rejoicing? (Luke 13:16)
20. What were they rejoicing over? (Luke 13:16)

#33 THE MAN WITH DROPSY (Luke 14:1-4)

Jesus went to house of one of the leaders of the Pharisees on the Sabbath to eat bread. How dare Jesus go into the house of a hypocrite and eat with him?! Of course, Jesus was known to rub elbows with sinners, gluttons, and drunkards, being accused of being one of them. (Luke 11:19)

1. Whose house did Jesus go into? (Luke 14:1)
2. Why did Jesus go into this house? (Luke 14:1)
3. What day was this? (Luke 14:1)

SABBATH: a day of religious observance and abstinence from work, kept by Jews from Friday evening to Saturday evening, and by most Christians on Sunday.

4. Who was in front of Jesus? (Luke 14:2)

DROPSY: hudrōpikos (hoo-dro-pik-os')= (as if looking watery); to be "dropsical": - have the dropsy. Dropsy was a condition of the swelling of the body due to retention of excessive liquid (water retention).

5. What question did Jesus ask the lawyers and Pharisees? (Luke 14:3, See Luke 13:15-16)
6. What did they do when Jesus asked them this question? (Luke 14:4)
7. In their silence what did Jesus do (again) on the Sabbath? (Luke 14:4)
8. When Jesus healed the man, what did He do to the man? (Luke 14:4)
9. What example did Jesus use when He healed a man on the Sabbath Day? (Luke 14:4)
10. What could the lawyers and Pharisees not do? (Luke 14:4)

34 TEN LEPERS (Luke 17:11-19)

Jesus was a travelling man. This time He was on the way to Jerusalem, and He was passing between Samaria and Galilee. This speaks to me of my hustle and bustle world as I am always going somewhere. The good news is that as Jesus was on the go, so was the Holy Spirit with Him.

1. Where did Jesus enter? (Luke 17:12)
2. Who met Him from a distance? (Luke 17:12)

NOTE: Leprosy was not a blessing; it was a curse. Leprosy is a chronic, curable infectious disease mainly causing skin lesions and nerve damage. Leprosy is caused by infection with the bacterium Mycobacterium leprae. It mainly affects the skin, eyes, nose, and peripheral nerves. Symptoms include light colored or red skin patches with reduced sensation, numbness and weakness in hands and feet. Leprosy can be cured with 6-12 months of multi-drug therapy. Early treatment avoids disability. (Information from a Google search).

Of course during the "Bible days" they did not have medications to deal with it, they either had it or they didn't. Jesus was a healer, so He healed these men who had leprosy. According to my Ryrie Study Bible notes, "see Leviticus 13 for seven forms of this skin disease, generally regarded not to be leprosy we know today. A leper was ceremonially unclean, had to live outside of the towns (a leper colony, mine), and had to cry "unclean" when other people came near. Leprosy serves as an illustration of sin, (however it was a real dis-ease and was consider to be a curse and not a blessing."

It is my observation on Isaiah 53:4 that Jesus not only bore spiritual problems like sin but also physical/spiritual problems like griefs, sorrows, afflictions, iniquities, sicknesses, and disease. The Amplified Bible says, "Surely He has borne our griefs (sicknesses, weaknesses, and distresses) and carried our sorrows {and} pains [of punishment], yet we [*ignorantly*] considered Him stricken, smitten, and afflicted by God [*as if with leprosy*]."(Isaiah 53:4, AMP) I like the phrase, "yet we [ignorantly] considered Him stricken, smitten, and afflicted by God [as with leprosy]." How many people ignorantly consider that we are made sick by God?

3. What did they raise when they saw Jesus? (Luke 17:13)

NOTE: A cry for mercy was a cry for healing of leprosy. A cry for mercy was a cry to be blessed and not cursed.

4. What did Jesus tell them to do? (Luke 17:14)

NOTE: Going to the priests was a requirement of Old Testament Law (Leviticus 10:33)

5. What happened "as they were going"? (Luke 17:14)

CLEANSED: katharizō (kath-ar-id'-zo) =From G2513; to cleanse (literally or figuratively): - (make) clean (-se), purge, purify. G2513: katharos (kath-ar-os') =Of uncertain affinity; clean (literally or figuratively): - clean, clear, pure.

NOTE: If they had not gone, there would be no healing. God can heal smack dab in the middle of religious rite, if the going is in obedience to the Lord. John 14:21 speaks of how to have a manifestation.

> "The person who has My commands (what He says to do) and keeps them (actually does them) is the one who [really] loves Me; and whoever [really] loves Me will be loved by My Father and I [too] will love him and will show (reveal, manifest) Myself to him. [I will let] (allow) Myself be clearly seen by him and make Myself real to him.]
> John 14:21, AMP

6. How many of them turned back when he saw that He was healed as he went? (Luke 17:15)
7. Was this one who saw that he had been healed (they all had been healed) did he glory God with a quiet voice? If not how did He glorify God for being healed? (Luke 17:15)
8. What was the man doing when he fell on His face at His feet? (Luke 17:16)
9. What was his heritage? (Luke 17:16)

SAMARITAN: a member of a people inhabiting Samaria

in biblical times, or of the modern community in the region of Nablus claiming descent from them, adhering to a form of Judaism accepting only its own ancient version of the Pentateuch as Scripture. (Google Dictionary)

NOTE: "The Samaritans were people who lived in what had been the Northern Kingdom of Israel. Samaria, the name of that kingdom's capital, was located between Galilee in the north and Judea in the south. The Samaritans were a racially mixed society with Jewish and pagan ancestry. Although they worshiped Yahweh as did the Jews, their religion was not mainstream Judaism. They accepted only the first five books of the Bible as canonical, and their temple was on Mount Gerazim instead of on Mount Zion in Jerusalem (John 4:20)." (www.catholic.com)

NOTE: Over the years I have heard taught that a "good Jew" would not travel through Samaria because the Samaritans were considered unclean. They would stop at the beginning of Samaria, cross over the river and cross again after they bypassed Samaria. Jesus, also a Jew, would go straight in to the heart of Samaria and minister to the Samaritan woman and others.

10. What did Jesus ask this one healed Samaritan? (Luke 17:17)

NOTE: One foreigner returned and thanked the Lord for healing him. Nine others who were healed did not return with thanks.

11. What did Jesus tell the foreigner to do? (Luke 17:19)

#35 SERVANT'S EAR (Luke 22:49-51)

Many times a sickness is internal. But God can even move

externally as with the servant's ear that Peter chopped off with a sword when they came to arrest Jesus as a result of the betrayal of Judas. A reattached ear ain't nothing for the miracle work then or now. Jesus had been praying fervently, agonizing in prayer about his pending passion of the cross to the point of His sweat became like drops of blood that fell on the ground. They may have been actual drops of blood where he prayed so hard that blood vessels broke in his head or sweat as large as drops of blood.

After He rose from prayer He found the disciples sawing logs and asked them about their sleep habits. Then He told them to rise and shine and pray not to enter into temptation.

1. Who came as He was speaking to sleeping beauties who came? (Luke 22:47)
2. Other than the crowd who came with them? (Luke 22:47)
3. What was the signal to let the men know which one was Jesus? (Luke 22:47, Matthew 26:47-54, Mark 14:43-50, John 18:3-11)
4. What did Jesus ask Judas? (Luke 22:48)

NOTE: The answer while not responded to was in the affirmative, yes.

NOTE: Petra had a song called *Judas Kiss*. The question was posed to Jesus about how did feel when the Prodigal left, and then ended with, it must feel just like Judas' kiss.

5. What did His disciple ask Him about what He wanted them to do? (Luke 22:48)
6. What did one of the disciples not wait for an answer, what did he do?
7. Who drew the sword and cut of the ear of the high priest's slave, Malchus? (John 18:10)

8. What was Jesus' response to Peter slicing of the ear? (Luke 22:51, John 18:11)

"So Jesus said to Peter, put the sword into the sheath; the cup which the Father has given Me, shall I not drink it."

John 18:11

NOTE: If the boys defended Jesus by violence, then they would be hindering the purpose that Jesus came, to ultimately destroy the works of the d-evil by delaying the death, burial and resurrection. (D.B.R. nothing more and nothing less)

#36 MAN COVERED WITH LEPROSY

Previously we saw Jesus healing ten lepers where 9 went away and one returned with thanksgiving. Now we see a man covered with leprosy.

1. Who was in one of the cities Jesus was in? (Luke 5:12)
2. What was the man covered with? (Luke 5:12)
3. What did the leper do when he saw Jesus? (Luke 5:12)
4. What statement did the leper make to Jesus about His will for him? (Luke 5:12)

"Lord IF you are willing, You can make me clean."

Luke 5:12

1. What two things did Jesus do with His hand? (Luke 5:12)
2. What did Jesus say as He touched the leper with His hand? (Luke 5:12)

"I am willing; be cleansed."

Luke 5:12

3. What was the cause and effect of Jesus laying His hand on the leper and speaking forth desire results? (Luke 5:12)
4. What did Jesus order him to not do? (Luke 5:12)
5. What did Jesus tell him to do? (Luke 5:12, Leviticus 13:49, Leviticus 14:2)

 # 37 MULTITUDES #10 (Luke 5:15)

As usual when Jesus was healing someone, the news spread.
1. What was the cause and effect when the news spread about the man's healing? (Luke 5:15)
2. What were the two things that the crowd gathered around Jesus for? (Luke 5:15)
3. After this healing, what did Jesus do? What was his habit that He often did? (Luke 5:16)

#38 VARIOUS PERSONS (Luke 13:31-32)

Jesus continued His mission in spite of opposition. When the Kingdom was concerned, even if told that He need to go and avoid death threats from Herod (Antipas), Jesus continued to minister to various people as needed.
1. As Jesus was teaching on the Kingdom of God and how some who thought they were chosen, would not make it in, who approached Jesus? (Luke 13:31)
2. What did they tell Jesus to do? (Luke 13:31)
3. What did Jesus call Herod? (Luke 13:31)

NOTE: Herod Antipas is described as a fox, known for its use of cunning deceit to achieve its aims. (Ryrie Study Bible note on Luke 13:31)

NOTE: Jesus uses the word "nevertheless" which implies that in spite of death threats He would stay on course.

4. What will Jesus do on "today and tomorrow"? (Luke 13:33)
5. What two things will Jesus be doing "today and tomorrow)? (Luke 13:33)
6. What would happen at the end of His journey? (Luke 13:33)
7. Where would Jesus perish (die)? (Luke 13:33)

#39 NOBLEMAN'S SON (John 4:46-53)

Again, Jesus is on the go and this time after two days He went forth from Samaria and ended up in Galilee. Jesus came into Cana, the site of His first miracle (changing water into wine) and the site of when His disciples first believed. (John 2:1-11) Now he was back in Cana where there would a second sign. (John 4:54)

1. What did Jesus testify? (John 4:45)
2. What did the Galileans do? (John 4:45)
3. Why did the Galileans receive Him? (John 4:45)
4. When did they see these thing? (John 4:45)
5. Who was in Cana and what was the problem? (John 4:45)
6. What had the royal official heard? (John 4:46)
7. What did the royal official do? (John 4:47)
8. How sick was the royal official's son? (John 4:47)
9. What did Jesus say about their belief? (John 4:48)
10. What was the royal official's response to Jesus? (John 4:49)
11. What did Jesus say to the royal official concerning the health of his son? (John 4:49)

12. What did the man do concerning the word that his son lives? (John 4:50)

13. What was the news from the slave when they met the royal official on his way home? (John 4:51)

14. What did the royal official inquire about from his slaves? (John 4:51)

15. What did they report to the royal official? (John 14:52)

16. What had left his son at the seventh hour, yesterday, exactly when Jesus had spoken the words to the royal official? (John 14:52-53)

17. What was the cause and effect on the royal official and on his household? (John 14:53)

 # 40 INVALID (John 5:2-9)

Jesus was a Jew and He was a good Jew. We see that Jesus was at a feast of the Jews and then He headed up to Jerusalem.

NOTE: For information on the gates of Jerusalem check out Nehemiah 3:1; Nehemiah 12:39. At the time of the rebuilding of the walls, there were five gates. Today in Jerusalem there are eight gates.

1. What was by a pool? (John 5:2)

2. What was this pool called in the Hebrew language? (John 5:2)

3. How many porticoes (porches) were there in this area? John 5:2)

4. Who did they lay in these area of pools? (John 5:2)

5. What were these sick, blind, lame and withered people waiting for? (John 5:3)

6. Who would come down and stir the waters? (John 5:4)

7. What would happen when the first one would step in the angel stirred waters? (John 5:4)

NOTE: These stirrings of the waters by angels happened in "certain seasons." (John 5:4)

8. What was made well? (John 5:4)

9. How long had one man been ill? (John 5:4)

NOTE: Can you imagine be sick for 38 years. We have seen a woman with an issue of blood for 12 years, someone bent over for 18 year, and now a man who had been ill for 38 years. We all know people with chronic illnesses, acute illness, hypochondriacs (Obsession with the idea of having a serious but undiagnosed medical condition) and psychosomatic illnesses, (of a physical illness or other condition caused or aggravated by a mental factor such as internal conflict or stress). Psychosomatic fits in with the makeup of mankind, where the psyche (mind, will, emotions aka soul) effects the soma (body, flesh, blood, bones, nerves, systems). (I Thessalonians 5:23)

10. When Jesus saw him lying there by the pool, what did Jesus know? (John 5:6)

NOTE: Either Jesus knew the man's personal history or had a word of knowledge.

11. What did Jesus say to him? (John 5:6)

NOTE: That may seem like an odd question. I mean who would not want to get well? There are many reasons why the man could have said no to being healed. He may have been sick so long that he had become institutionalized like a long term prisoner. Sometimes, the prisoner has been imprisoned for so long that the natural feeling was to be in prison. Releasing the prisoner from the bondage of prison would seem odd. Another reason would be all the attention and pity that the sick person has received over the years. Another reason, more likely in this age, would be the financial benefit of a disability check coming in every month.

1. How did the sick man respond? (John 5:7)
2. What did Jesus tell the man to do? (John 5:8)
3. How soon did the man become well? (John 5:9)
4. What did the man do? (John 5:9)
5. What day did this healing/miracle take place? (John 5:9)

#41 MAN BORN BLIND (John 9:1-11)

Wherever Jesus went, he caused an eruption of praise or generated hatred to the point of people wanting to and trying to kill Him. There was a group of people who picked up stones to throw at Him, but Jesus hid himself and went out of the temple. Yes, the ones who wanted to stone the Messiah were the ones waiting for the Messiah. (John 8:1-59)

1. Who did Jesus see when He passed by those who wanted to kill Him? (John 9:1)
2. The disciples who also saw the blind man asked Jesus a question, what was that question? (John 9:2)

NOTE: The thought process was that if someone was sick it must have been caused by someone sinning, either his parents or the man himself. Since he was born blind, that meant he had sinned and done something to cause his blindness, or his parents had done something to cause the blind birth. I know that "all have sinned and fallen short of the glory of God." (Romans 3:10) I know that there is none (not even a baby) righteous, no not one." (Romans 6:23) I know that because Adam sinned and because of that "so death was passed to all men/mankind because all have sinned." (Romans 5:12) But, the little baby did nothing before he was born. Jesus broke through the tradition of men to the heart of the matter.

3. Who did Jesus say was the cause of the blindness? (John 9:3)

4. Why was the man blind? (John 9:3)

NOTE: So that the works of God may be seen. The work of God was not sickness but healing. Remember Acts 10:38, "You know of Jesus of Nazareth how God (the Father) anointed Him/Jesus (for the purpose of destroying the works of the d-evil) and how He went about (for three years) doing good (good works not bad works) and healing (not making sick or blind since birth) all who were harassed and oppressed by the d-evil (not by God) for God was with Him/Jesus (Immanuel God with us).

5. What must we do? (John 9:4)

6. How long must we do those works? (John 9:4)

7. What was coming and what would be the work accomplished? (John 9:4)

8. What was Jesus as long as He was in the world? (John 9:5)

NOTE: In the Beatitudes (the Attitudes that we need to be having) Jesus taught that we are the light of the world (in the darkness of the world) (Matthew 5:14) so we (the lights), would not be hidden or covered by a basket.

9. How are we supposed to let our light be seen? (Matthew 5:16)

10. What should be seen? (Matthew 5:16)

11. When people see your good works what will they do? (Matthew 5:16)

12. After Jesus said that He was the light in the world, what did He do? (John 9:6)

13. What did Jesus make out of the spit on the ground? (John 9:6)

14. What did He do with the spit and dirt that was made into clay? (John 9:6)

NOTE: You have heard the phrase, "Here's mud in your eye." Jesus the Optometrist practiced the method of improving vision.

15. What did Jesus tell the man to do after He put spit mud in his eyes? (John 9:6)
16. What did the man do? (John 9:7)
17. How did the blind man come back? (John 9:7)
18. What was the response when the neighbors (who knew the man as a beggar) saw him? (John 9:8)

NOTE: There was not a unanimous decision about if this was the blind man or not the blind man.

19. What did the former blind man keep saying? (John 9:9)
20. What did the Pharisees ask him? (John 9:10)
21. What was the former blind man's answer? (John 9:11)

NOTE: For the full story read John 9:1-41

#42 LAZARUS (John 11:1-44)

Other than Jesus there were only three others who were raised from the dead. (1) The widow in Nain, her son (2) Jairus' daughter (3) Lazarus.

1. Who was sick? (John 11:1)
2. Where did he live? (John 11:1)
3. Who were his sisters? (John 11:1)
4. Which sister had anointed Jesus with ointment and wiped His feet with her hair? (John 11:2)
5. Who did the sisters send word to? (John11:3)
6. What did they say about Jesus' relationship with Lazarus? (John 11:3)
7. What did Jesus say about this sickness? (John 11:4)
8. What was this sickness not to end in? (John 11:4)

9. What was the sickness for? (John 11:4)

NOTE: Once again we see that sickness was not for the glory of God but healing was.

NOTE: Notice that even though Jesus said that Lazarus sickness was not to end in death, it did end in death.

10. What was the glory of God for? (John 11:4)

GLORIFIED: doxazō (dox-ad'-zo) =From G1391; to render (or esteem) glorious (in a wide application): - (make) glorify (-ious), full of (have) glory, honour, magnify. G1391: doxa (dox'-ah) = From the base of G1380; glory (as very apparent), in a wide application (literally or figuratively, objectively or subjectively): - dignity, glory (-ious), honour, praise, worship. G1380: dok-eh'-o (A prolonged form of a primary verb dokō (used only as an alternate in certain tenses; compare the base of G1166); of the same meaning; to think; by implication to seem (truthfully or uncertainly): - be accounted, (of own) please (-ure), be of reputation, seem (good), suppose, think, trow.

11. Who did Jesus love? (John 11:5)
12. How long did Jesus stay in the place where He was after He heard that Lazarus was sick? (John 11:6)
13. After that what did He say to the disciples? (John 11:7)

NOTE: Jesus would be going back to the place where the Jews were just trying to stone Him. The disciples took note of this.

14. What did the disciples ask Jesus about the return trip? (John 11:8)

NOTE: John 11:9-10 gives Jesus' reasoning about his safety which was that as long as He was walking in the light, walking in the Father's will, He would be OK.

15. What did He tell the disciples about the reason for going back? (John 11:11)

16. What did Jesus say about Lazarus' death? (John 11:11)

17. What did Jesus tell them He was going to do? (John 11:11)

NOTE: The disciples did not understand that when Jesus said "sleep" he was talking about "death." They wonder if he was asleep, then he would wake up and Jesus would not need to go back. (John 11:12-13)

18. How did Jesus clarify to them what He was saying? (John 11:14)

19. Why did Jesus tell them that He was glad that He was not there (to heal him)? (John 11:15)

20. What did Thomas (the doubter) Didymus say to his fellow disciples? (John 11:16)

21. When Jesus came what did He find? (John 11:17)

22. How many days had Lazarus already been in the tomb? (John 11:18)

23. How far was Bethany away from Jerusalem? (John 11:18)

NOTE: It was only a one day journey. It seems to me that Jesus purposely delayed the journey to make sure that Lazarus was good and dead and smelled ripe with death. Why? I don't know, but it would be no doubt that Lazarus was dead and no doubt that Jesus raised him from the dead.

24. What had the many Jews come to do? (John 11:19)

25. Who went out to meet Jesus and who stayed at home? (John 11:20)

26. What did Martha say to Jesus concerning what would have happened if he had been there? (John 11:21)

27. What did Martha say to Jesus about even though Lazarus had died, what Jesus could do? (John 11:22)

28. What did Jesus say would happen to her brother, Lazarus? (John 11:23)
29. How did Martha misunderstand about what Jesus meant about Lazarus rising from the dead? (John 11:24)

JESUS' VIEW OF WHO HE WAS

Jesus knew that He was not just a mere mortal man from Nazareth. He knew that He was the only begotten Son of God that He was God manifested in the flesh, that He was God the great I AM.

"Jesus said to her, I am the resurrection and the life; he who believes in Me will live even if he dies (like Lazarus)."
John 11:25
with addition mine

30. After Jesus told Martha who He was, what did He say would happen to those who believe in Him? (John 11:26)
31. Jesus then asked Martha a question that He asks every one of us? (John 11:26)
NOTE: John 3:16 speaks of people believing having ever-lasting life.
32. What was Martha's response? (John 11:27)
NOTE: This was the same revelation that Peter had from the Father in Matthew 16:16 when Jesus asked the disciples,

"...but who do you say that I am."
Matthew 16:15

"Simon Peter answered, You are the Christ, the Son of the Living God."

Matthew 16:16

JESUS: Iēsous (ee-ay-sooce') =Of Hebrew origin [H3091]; Jesus (that is, Jehoshua), the name of our Lord and two (three) other Israelites: - Jesus. H3O91: yehôshûa yehôshûa (yeh-ho-shoo'-ah, yeh-ho-shoo'-ah) = Jehovah-saved; Jehoshua (that is, Joshua), the Jewish leader: - Jehoshua, Jehoshuah, Joshua.

CHRIST: Christo (khris-tos')=From G5548; anointed, that is, the Messiah, an epithet of Jesus: - Christ. G5548: chriō (khree'-o) =through the idea of contact; to smear or rub with oil, that is, (by implication) to consecrate to an office or religious service: - anoint.

33. What did Martha do when she made this confession? (John 11:28)
34. When Mary heard that Jesus was calling for her secretly, what did Mary do? (John 11:29)
35. Had Jesus come into the village yet, and if not where was He? (John 11:30)
36. What did the Jews who were consoling Mary (professional mourners) do when they saw her leave so quickly? (John 11:31)
37. Where did the consolers think she was going? (John 11:31)
38. What did Mary do when she came to Jesus? (John 11:32)
39. What did she say to Jesus? (John 11:32)
40. What was Jesus' response when He saw Mary grieving and the others weeping? (John 11:33)
41. What did Jesus want to know? (John 11:34)

42. What did Jesus do? (John 11:35)

NOTE: There was a difference in Jesus weeping and Mary, Martha, and the crowd weeping.

WEEPING: klaiō (klah'-yo)=Of uncertain affinity; to sob, that is, wail aloud (whereas G1145 is rather to cry silently): - bewail. weep. This is what Mary and Martha and the other mourners were doing.

WEPT: dakruō (dak-roo'-o)= to shed tears (silently, mine) : - weep. This is what Jesus did compared to the wailing the others were doing. Both were emotions, but Jesus' emotions were under control even though He was deeply moved in spirit and was troubled.

NOTE: There were mixed emotions about Jesus from the crowd. One group noted who Jesus wept said it was sign of how much he loved Lazarus. The other group complained about Jesus not being able to keep Lazarus from dying but could open eyes of the blind.

43. What was Jesus again? (John 11:38)
44. Where was Lazarus buried? (John 11:38)
45. What did Jesus tell the people to do to the stone that sealed the cave where Lazarus was buried? (John 11:39-40)
46. What was Martha's response to Jesus' request? (John 11:39)
47. What was Jesus' response to Martha about the fact that Lazarus "stinketh"? (John 11:39)
48. What was Mary, Martha and the crowd about to see? (John 11:40)

NOTE: Sometimes you have to endure the stench to see the miracle.

49. What did they do to the stone? (John 11:41)

NOTE: Sometimes (most of the time, if not all the time) you have to move in obedience to see a miracle. Like Mary and the water/wine situation.

50. What did Jesus thank the Father for? (John 11:41)

51. If Jesus knew the Father what He had prayed why was He raising his eyes and thank the Father that He had heard Him? (John 11:41)

"So do not be like them; for our Father knows what you need before you ask."

Matthew 6:8

NOTE: The Father knew that Lazarus had died and knew that Jesus was going to pray for a resurrection.

52. Why was Jesus praying out loud if He knew the Father had heard His prayer? (John 11:42)

53. What did Jesus cry out with a loud voice? (John 11:43)

"...LAZARUS, COME FORTH."

John 11:43

54. What was the cause and effect of Jesus speaking those specific words to Lazarus?" (John 11:44)

NOTE: It has been said that if Jesus had not used Lazarus' name, that all of the dead people would have come out.

55. How did Lazarus come out? What was his hands and feet bound with? What was wrapped around his face with? (John 11:44)

56. What two things did Jesus tell those around Lazarus to do? (John 11:45)

NOTE: While Jesus had resurrected Lazarus from the dead (the ultimate healing), God still used people to unbind him and let him go. This is a vivid picture of people getting saved and God using human beings to help people get loose from the things binding them and letting them go into freedom.

That completes 42 incidences of Jesus healing and delivering people on earth as it is in heaven. There may be more but this is all that I could find.

"Therefore many other signs Jesus also performed in the presence of the disciples which are not written in this book; but these have been written so that you may believe that Jesus is the Christ, the Son of God; and that believing you may have life in His name."

John 20:30-31

FINAL THOUGHTS. FINALLY

Well, you have just finished *On Earth As It Is In Heaven*. I started the book in the introduction by saying that I was approaching healing from a biased perspective. I am ending the book with the same biased perspective that Jesus is the Healer and that the Father's will has not changed. If it was God's will to heal yesterday, then it is God's will to heal today, and it is God's will to heal, yes forever.

I hope that you have taken time and gone through the workbook chapter and looked up the Scriptures and wrote your answers. I believe that as you have heard the Word concerning healing that faith has come and you have been encouraged concerning not only healing but every area of your life.

ABOUT THE AUTHOR

Rodney Boyd is first and foremost a follower of Jesus Christ. He is also a husband, dad and speech-language pathologist. Rodney holds a Master's Degree in Education with emphasis in Speech Communication and has been a practicing Speech-Language Pathologist since 1993. He holds a 2nd degree Black Belt in Wado Ryu Karate; has a passion for music of all styles; and enjoys writing, teaching the Word of God.

Rodney has been married to his high school sweetheart, Brenda, for more than 40 years and together they have one son, Phillip, a daughter-in-law, Jamie, and one granddaughter, Emerson Grace (How Sweet The Sound) Boyd.

Boyd bases his life on Colossians 3:17, "And whatever you do in word or deed, do all in the name of the Lord Jesus, giving thanks through Him to God the Father."

Connect with Rodney on line at:
www.rodneylewisboyd.com

RODNEY BOYD

Never Run a Dead Data
Pro-Verb Ponderings
Speaking and Hearing the Word of God
Chewing the Daily Cud, Vols 1-4
Written That You May Believe

WORDCRAFTS PRESS

Morning Mist: *Stories from the Water's Edge*
    by Barbie Loflin

Youth Ministry is Easy! *and 9 other lies*
    by Aaron Shaver

Chronicles of a Believer
    by Don McCain

Pondering(s)
    by Wayne Berry

www.wordcrafts.net

Made in the USA
Middletown, DE
01 November 2022

13851860R00126